Copyright © 2024 by Dylan and Friends Publishing Company

All rights reserved.

No part of this book may be reproduced or transmitted in any form or by any means, electronic or mechanical, including photocopying, recording, or by an information storage and retrieval system - except by a reviewer who may quote brief passages in a review to be printed in a magazine or newspaper - without permission in writing from the publisher.

Library of Congress Control Number: 2024916063

Hardback ISBN: 978-1-959215-21-9

eBook ISBN: 978-1-959215-22-6

DEAR DYLAN'S DOG SQUAD

WISDOM AND WAGS ON PET OWNERSHIP

KATHLEEN TROY

CONTENTS

Books by Kathleen Troy	vii
Prologue	1
Chapter 1	3
Me! Pick Me!	
Chapter 2	19
Only Young Once	
Chapter 3	39
Wanting Isn't Getting	
Chapter 4	59
Road Trip!	
Chapter 5	73
Oh Wow! Chow!	
Chapter 6	89
Training the Humans	
Chapter 7	109
Show Time!	
Chapter 8	113
A Little Help Here	
Chapter 9	129
Forever in Our Hearts	
About Dylan Easter Troy	135
Acknowledgments	137
About the Author	139
Stay Informed	141

BOOKS BY KATHLEEN TROY

Dylan's Dog Squad Series

Dylan's Dilemma

Dylan's Dream

Dylan's Villain

Dylan's Hawaiian Ghost ('O ka 'uhane Hawai'i 'o Dylan)

Dylan's Nose Knows

*Coming soon:*Dylan's Millions

Dear Dylan's Dog Squad: Wisdom and Wags on Pet Ownership

Never Believe Series

Never Believe in Luck Twice

(Prologue/short story to Never Believe a Lie Twice)

Never Believe a Lie Twice

Never Believe a Con Artist Twice

Coming soon: Never Believe in Fate Twice

To Dylan,
Semper eris numerus unus.
(You'll always be number one.)

Casey and Sumo,
It's my job to take care of you.
Don't make me look bad.
Dylan

PROLOGUE

DEAR FRIENDS,

When Dylan's Dog Squad isn't busy solving mysteries, catching bad guys and doing search and rescue, we love visiting schools, working with organizations such as Scouts, and participating in charitable events. It's always exciting to meet new people and we are often asked about our two favorite topics, dogs and dog training.

Dear Dylan's Dog Squad is inspired by your questions. If you have a question, please contact us. In return, we will send you a free Dylan's Dog Squad bandana.

As always, Dylan's Dog Squad is grateful for your love and support. We couldn't do any of this without you.

Happy reading!
Casey, Dylan, and Sumo
aka Dylan's Dog Squad

ONE

ME! PICK ME!

DEAR FRIENDS,

You are at the shelter and two soulful brown eyes look back at you. A whine escapes and... you are hooked. Before you adopt, think twice and please carefully consider what adoption will mean.

It's been said that having a dog is like having a child who never grows up. Not true, you say? Think again.

- What will it be like to have a pet completely dependent on you for their entire life? For some dogs, that may be twenty years.
- What would happen if you moved, married, had children?
- What would you do if a family member were allergic to the dog? Or they couldn't get along with the dog? Or they lost interest in the dog?
- Some dogs require dedicated exercise, frequent grooming, or medical treatment. What would happen if your financial picture changed?

No problem, you say. Great! You may be the perfect dog owner if you...

- can share your home with a dog that sheds, tracks in mud, never picks up his toys, howls in the middle of the night and regards everything you own as his.
- think caring for a dog for the next two decades isn't such a long time.
- are thrilled when sloppy canine kisses on your face wake you up instead of an annoying alarm clock.
- can spend a chunk of your disposable income on vet bills and endless pet toys.
- enjoy having three thousand photos—all of your dog.
- will spay or neuter your dog, knowing it is for their best interest.

- will microchip your dog and ensure up-to-date contact info is on his collar and harness.
- insist your devoted fur baby goes with you if you must relocate.
- realize that being a dog owner is the best job you will ever have.

Dylan's Dog Squad

Dear Dylan's Dog Squad,
What is the best dog to have?

Thanks,
Cindy

Dear Cindy,
Yours.

Dylan's Dog Squad

Dear Dylan's Dog Squad,
Two years ago, I visited a shelter and fell in love with an adorable one-year-old St. Bernard puppy. I brought her home and named her Stella. Now Stella weighs one hundred fifty pounds and has paws the size of dinner plates. I still love her, but I feel like my house is shrinking. What do I do?

Help,
Michael

DEAR MICHAEL,

What to do isn't the question. The question is, Why didn't you do your research? When you met Stella, you knew her breed.

Even at one year, Stella's big paws were visible. It's common knowledge that puppies grow into their paws and St. Bernards aren't exactly the ballerinas of the canine world. Their big paws are necessary, providing support and helping to maintain the dog's balance just the way feet support a human's body.

It's not Stella's fault she grew up. Think about this. You grew up and your parents still love you. It seems you have a choice here: Find suitable living arrangements for you and Stella or find a suitable home for her. If you choose the latter, consider a rescue organization, such as Sunny Saints, Southern California St. Bernard Rescue. They are a nonprofit organization and may be contacted at: sunnysaints.org or **info@sunnysaints.org**.

Good luck to you and Stella.

Dylan's Dog Squad

DEAR DYLAN'S DOG SQUAD,

Mia, my eight-year-old daughter, begs me for a dog day and night. I'm thinking about getting her one to teach her responsibility. What do you think?

Sincerely,
Amy

DEAR AMY,

Get a dog when *you* want the responsibility.

Sure, kids and dogs are a natural combination. We bet Mia has tugged on your hand (and your heartstrings) and has given you the big, wide-eyed stare, followed by, *"Mo-m,* can I have a dog? *Please."* You're not sure you should answer "yes" because you know all too well dogs are a lifelong commitment.

Some dogs live to age twenty. Dogs are also a big expense: food, vet bills, dog training—the list goes on.

Then you remember growing up with your family dog and what it meant to you. You think, *Why not?*

Imagine this: It begins so well. Mia walks the dog, shows it off to everyone and the dog soon becomes her new best friend. Then the dog poops on Mia's bedroom rug and she steps in it while getting out of bed. Or, shudder, Mia takes the dog for a walk and has to carry *and* use a poop bag. (What will her friends say if she is seen picking up pup poop?) Or the dog mistakes Mia's new headband for a chew toy?

Or Mia grows older, her interest wanes and then what? You take over.

Think about this carefully. Every adopted pet deserves a forever home.

Dylan's Dog Squad

DEAR DYLAN'S DOG SQUAD

Dear Dylan's Dog Squad,

I've put off getting a dog because I wanted the time to be right. I'm now lucky to have a secure job that allows me to work from home. My house has a large, fenced in backyard and I love to walk every day. The trouble is even though I know I want a dog I don't really know that much about them. (I've never had one.) I don't want to make a mistake, so I could use a little help here. Should I get a pedigree dog? I hear mutts are great.

Thanks,
Simon

Dear Simon,

Lucky you! Lucky dog-to-be!

Purchasing a pedigree from a reputable breeder can have its advantages if you are in the market for a certain type of dog. Mutts have their own charm, too, and many experts will tell you they are less likely to have health problems.

Start by honestly answering these questions.

1. What do you want? There's nothing wrong with being attracted to a certain type of dog. Small, medium, big, or gigantic? Furry or smooth coat? Do you like the happy, yappy kind or prefer the silent type?

2. What do you need? If you have allergies research dogs that are considered to be hypoallergenic. Are you looking for a constant companion or a dog who is happy just to be in the same room with you?
3. Will maintenance be an issue? Some dogs require daily brushing to keep their fur from matting as well as regular trips to the groomer. If that's the case, you need to consider the expense.
4. Who else lives in your house? Is that someone an adult? How does he or she feel about a new addition? If you live with children, what are their ages?

When you've answered these questions, start your research. Most dogs were originally bred to hunt birds, other animals, or vermin. If you select one of these breeds, chances are your dog will want to run and dig. Other dogs were bred to work on farms and have herding instincts, meaning they like to crowd you when you walk or even nip at your heels if you aren't going fast enough. Adults may find this difficult, and kids may find this scary. Others worked as guard dogs and to this day will remain fiercely loyal to one owner or their families while being aggressive to outsiders.

The thing is, even after many years of domesticity, natural instincts such as stalking or herding will remain. Pay attention to advice such as, "May not be a good choice for first time dog owners." Translated, that means the dog may have high energy levels or is high maintenance or prone to health problems.

This is an exciting time for you. When you make your choice, do so with "providing a forever home" in mind. Choose wisely.

Dylan's Dog Squad

DEAR DYLAN'S DOG SQUAD,

I'm thirty-three years old, have never had a dog but I've always wanted one. On the plus side my home is large and has a fenced in yard, I love outdoor activities, and I'm self-employed at home. The only reason I haven't gotten a dog is because sometimes I get an allergic reaction when I'm around one. I talked to my doctor, and he suggested a hypoallergenic dog. I like all dogs. Is a little dog more hypoallergenic than a big one?

Malcolm

DEAR MALCOLM,

The truth is, there are no one hundred percent hypoallergenic dogs, dog breeds, or mixed breeds. Some breeds are just less allergenic than others. People are actually allergic to dander, which is attached to pet hair, not to the dog itself.

Here is a list of dogs considered to be hypoallergenic.

- Bichon Frisé
- Giant Schnauzer
- American Hairless Terrier
- Soft-coated Wheaten Terrier
- Lagotto Romagnolo
- Affenpinscher
- Goldendoodle
- Poodle (most popular)
- Portuguese Water Dog
- Maltese
- Kerry Blue Terrier
- Yorkshire Terrier
- Basenji
- Peruvian Inca Orchid

- Xoloitzcuintli
- Chinese Crested Dog
- Irish Water Spaniel
- Bedlington Terrier
- Coton de Tulear
- Havanese
- Shih Tzu
- Bolognese
- Australian Terrier
- Afghan Hound

Before you adopt do your research and then seek the advice of your doctor and a veterinarian. Also, just because a dog is hypoallergenic doesn't mean grooming will be minimal. Many of the breeds listed require daily brushing to avoid matting and routine trips to the groomer.

You have many wonderful dogs to choose from. Take your time.

Dylan's Dog Squad

DEAR DYLAN'S DOG SQUAD

DEAR DYLAN'S DOG SQUAD,

I only know three things about Roscoe: he's big, a gentle giant and high energy.

My vet thinks he is four years old. People always ask me why he is my dog. It's a mystery to me, too. I've always liked small dogs, but we met and that was it. Now I couldn't imagine life without him.

Roscoe is content to sit for about two minutes. After that I can almost see the wheels spinning in his head. We jog, use the treadmill together and go for long walks. I even got him a bike trailer so he can go on bike rides with me. Thanks to Roscoe, I've lost thirty pounds and have never been in better shape.

Two weeks ago, we started an Agility Class. Roscoe loves it. It's good for him so I like it too, except for the people.

They are fanatics. One guy will only give his dog commands in German. One lady dresses her dog up in booties and (she told me) Donna Karan outfits. During breaks they talk about their dogs' pedigrees. They've even had their dogs' DNA done. A few have made snobby remarks about Roscoe and have told mutt jokes. I don't want him to hear, so we use break time to relax by ourselves.

I don't think I can take six more weeks of this.

Seth

DEAR SETH,

You can because you will do it for Roscoe. In fact, we think you get the good daddy award!

As long as Roscoe is enjoying himself you can too by knowing you are doing something good for him. Roscoe will be focusing on you during the class so keep your mood enthusiastic and your face happy. After class, ask the instructor about upcoming classes. Most dog training facilities offer a wide variety of classes, anything from training to socialization. There's nothing to say you can't take a class just for fun! Different classes will have different people and dogs.

It's all part of the big adventure. Get the most out of it.

Dylan's Dog Squad

DEAR DYLAN'S DOG SQUAD,

I'm a successful businesswoman and own an ad agency with forty employees, working eighty hours a week and loving it. I never understood people whose lives centered around telling cutesy stories about their kids and plaguing you with pictures of them.

For thirty-seven years, I managed to escape marriage, having kids, joining a homeowner's association and volunteer work. I've never had a reason for a pet and once turned down a free Betta fish.

Last October after a meeting in Las Vegas, I was hurrying to catch a chartered flight. In the shadows I glimpsed a dog on the runway. She was dirty, her fur was matted, and her front paw was bleeding. She looked half starved. I asked the flight crew about her. They said she'd been hanging around and didn't belong to anyone.

When I checked to see if she had a collar, she licked my hand. I couldn't leave her behind so I took her, thinking she would be better off at a shelter.

I learned shelters are overcrowded and I also learned what happens when a pet doesn't get adopted. Grim.

She became Carly.

She goes to work with me every day and is my life. I (seriously) have about twenty-five hundred pictures of Carly on my phone and show them to everyone—even though she is right there. I admit she has saved me from being selfish, but I fear I'm becoming one of "those people." What do you think?

Trish

DEAR TRISH,

We think you should send us pictures! Congrats!

Dylan's Dog Squad

Dear Dylan's Dog Squad,

On my fiftieth birthday my grown kids gave me a surprise birthday party and a (surprise!) Golden American Cocker Spaniel puppy. She came with a six-month supply of everything she'll need, plus ID tags. Since *The Princess Bride* is my favorite movie, I wasn't too surprised when my kids told me they named her Princess Buttercup.

She loves to go everywhere with me, is almost old enough to be microchipped and we will be starting training soon. Everyone keeps asking me what her name is. The truth is, I'm six foot six and weigh two hundred and twenty pounds. I feel ridiculous calling her Princess Buttercup. It sticks in my throat. I thought about using her initials but calling out Pee Bee isn't much better. I don't want to hurt my kids' feelings either. I'd prefer the name Mandy.

Ken

Dear Ken,

Since you don't want to opt for the truth, try opting for logic. Most dogs respond better to names that are one or two syllables.

A gift is one that is freely given. Mandy is a nice name and she's your dog. Happy birthday!

Dylan's Dog Squad

DEAR DYLAN'S DOG SQUAD

Dear Dylan's Dog Squad,

In my life I've had two cats that lived to be twenty-two, another that lived to be eighteen and another that lived to be sixteen. I had a German Shepherd that lived to be thirteen and two Poodles that lived to be fourteen. When Sneakers, my Basset Hound, passed away, he was sixteen. I'm grateful for all the years Sneakers gave me but without him there is a hole in my heart.

I miss him dreadfully. Since he passed away, I'm constantly asked if I will get another dog. I would love one! But I'm seventy-three and I have absolutely no one to take a dog if something were to happen to me. Still, whenever I see a furry face, I feel myself weaken. What do you think?

Elizabeth

Dear Elizabeth,

Although not a pleasant thought, everyone who considers adopting any pet should also consider Plan B: What If Something Should Happen to Me?

Have you thought of fostering? Some foster agencies specialize in dog breeds, or mutts or a certain size. You know yourself best and what you can accommodate. There are many fur babies who could use a kind heart and gentle touch until they get their forever home.

You may be just what a dog needs even if it is temporary. And you would be helping yourself too. It seems to us that your abundant heart has room for one more.

Dylan's Dog Squad

TWO

ONLY YOUNG ONCE

DEAR FRIENDS,

Here are some of the most popular reasons for getting a dog:

- **Companionship** – It's no fun being alone. Dogs provide a great deal of comfort and empathy. A dog will tilt his head when you talk to him, letting you know he is enjoying the conversation. A dog also tends to agree with you.
- **Exercise** – All dogs require exercise. Since you will be on the other end of the leash you will be getting some too.
- **You always wanted one.** Who hasn't?
- **A dog loves you no matter what.** It's true. A dog doesn't care if you are five pounds overweight, if you have a minimum wage job or are a CEO.
- **Protection** – Dogs have excellent hearing. Often, they know if someone is on your doorstep before your security camera does.
- **Health benefits** – Many experts claim the mere act of petting a dog can lower your blood pressure significantly.
- **A dog will teach responsibility.** Maybe. It really depends on who is supposed to be learning the lesson here—an adult or a child.

These are all excellent reasons for you. Are they excellent reasons for the dog?

Sadly, many people like *the idea* of getting a dog much better than they like *actually having* a dog. While the benefits of dog ownership are enormous, so are the responsibilities. Do your research and only commit when you are confidant you can provide a forever home.

Dylan's Dog Squad

DEAR DYLAN'S DOG SQUAD

Dear Dylan's Dog Squad,

My wife told me we're going shopping for our new puppy and showed me a "must have" list that is longer than Santa Claus's Christmas list. There's no way one little dog could possibly use all that stuff. What do we really need?

Jonathan

Dear Jonathan,

Your veterinarian is the expert and can help you make decisions about the following:

- **Puppy food** – You have many choices: dry or wet food, small breed formulas and large breed formulas. The right food will be based on your pup's nutritional needs. Your vet will tell you how much to feed and how often. Most importantly do not let your pup self-feed. By monitoring his food, you will know how much he is eating and how often. Also, you will need to take him out to go potty after meals. This will give you the chance to observe whether the food agrees with him.
- **Food and water bowls** – Begin with smaller bowls. As your pup grows increase the size of the bowls. Because pups tend to step on or in their bowls and knock them over, the bowls need to be sturdy and easy to clean. Do not let your pup self-feed but always have fresh water available for him to drink during the day. To avoid accidents in the house, take him out after eating and drinking.
- **Collar, ID tags, and microchipping** – No matter how well-behaved your pup is, the chance of him getting lost always exists. Safeguard against this by getting a collar and ID tag before you bring your pup home. (In fact,

many municipalities require a proper collar and an ID tag with current contact information on dogs at all times.) Pups grow quickly. Check his collar often to ensure you can put two fingers under it easily. Microchipping is a reliable method of identification. Your vet can explain the procedure to you and advise when your pup is old enough to have it done.

- **Crates** – They can provide your pup a safe place to sleep and to go to—kind of like his own puppy clubhouse. Choose a collapsible crate (you can use it when you travel too) that allows your pup to stand up, turn around and stretch out on his side. A comfy firm pillow or mattress is a must. Even if your pup will grow into a large dog, start with a small crate. If it is too large, your pup will not understand why he is there and may use a corner for elimination.
- **Bed** – Pups like a comfy firm bed just like we do. It will make him happy to know he has something that is his. You can also train him to go lie down if he becomes too excited when there is a lot of commotion in the house or if you are having a social event.
- **Toys** – Yes! Puppies have puppy teeth and like to chew because it feels good. Select chew toys, avoiding anything with parts, fuzzy bits, or sharp edges. It's amazing what those sharp teeth can take apart and how quickly. Beware of balls that are too small. They can be swallowed or become lodged in his throat, causing him to choke. Pups love plastic, so beware. Keep all bags and wrappings off the floor and out of his reach. They can cause suffocation.

Never give your pup toys that look like shoes. They can't tell a toy from your shoe. They taste the same! Never give him any socks or items of clothing to play with. That is too confusing. They can't tell a ratty T-shirt from your favorite leather jacket.

Always supervise your pup's playtime. As soon as a toy breaks down, get rid of it. Loose pieces, yarn and parts can cause choking.

- **Treats should be yummy and nutritious.** They are useful for training and for rewarding for good behavior. Treats should be small enough to be gulped but don't feed him too many. Dogs, just like humans, need to follow a good diet. Ask your vet what your dog's caloric intake should be. Only ten percent of his calories should come from treats.
- **Grooming** – You may opt for a professional groomer and that is good. They can bathe, trim nails and groom as required. Still, you will need supplies for every day. What you need depends on your dog's breed. Even shorthaired dogs need regular brushing, shampoo and conditioner for a bath and a nail trimmer. Longhaired dogs may need a variety of brushes and combs and need to be groomed daily to avoid matting.

It is helpful to start by showing your pup the brush and then running it gently over his body and ears. This will help him get used to it. It sounds silly but let him watch when you brush your hair. Then let him sniff your brush. Repeat the process by gently running his brush over his body and ears. Increase the time gradually.

If your dog has floppy ears, they may need regular cleaning to avoid infections. Your veterinarian can show you how and prescribe the proper treatment.

Cleaning supplies can be very difficult to choose. Housetraining takes patience and time. Before accidents in the home happen visit the pet aisle at your local pet store or ask your vet's advice. It's important to find an enzymatic cleaner that will remove pet stains as well as pet odors. Use of these products will prevent your pup from repeatedly marking his spot. Always keep these supplies in a pet proofed cabinet or on a high shelf.

You're ready!

Dylan's Dog Squad

DEAR DYLAN'S DOG SQUAD,

My wife's favorite sister just got Angus, a Boston Terrier puppy. I know it takes time to train puppies, and Angus is cute... but I dread his visits. So far Angus has peed on our cashmere handwoven rug, the drapes and all the baseboards in the house—several times. He must be dehydrated when he leaves. On his last visit he christened the leg of my Steinway grand piano. I'm afraid to complain to my wife. I have to live with her.

Christopher

DEAR CHRISTOPHER,

You are wise to realize you have to live with your wife but you do not have to live with her favorite sister. The next time your sister-in-law comes for a visit, kindly but firmly suggest she keep Angus on a leash and with her at all times. If that doesn't do it, move the visit outdoors. We're sure the plants won't mind Angus's contribution.

Dylan's Dog Squad

Dear Dylan's Dog Squad,

We want to throw our puppy a welcome home party when we bring him home from the shelter. What should we do first?

Samuel and Rebecca

Dear Samuel and Rebecca,

Stop. Leaving his life behind, even if it is for a better one, will be stressful on your new pup. A party would add to that stress. Instead, consider the following:

Tips to Make Both of You Happy

- Until this moment your pup has been confined to a kennel or shelter. Suddenly he is in a new place with new smells and sounds. This can be exciting and frightening all at the same time. Introduce him to your home one room at a time.
- Choose a designated outdoor potty area. When he relieves himself say a command that you will always use, like, "Go potty." Since housetraining is always involved with a new puppy, you can encourage the learning by giving a tiny yummy treat each time he goes potty.
- Do meet and greets with your family, one member at a time. Be careful with young children. They will be as excited as your new pup. Tell them to sit quietly and pet your pup or hold it quietly on their laps.
- Wait a few days before you introduce your new pup to outsiders.

- Introduce other family pets carefully. If they become agitated separate them from your puppy. (Remember they were there first. They may not be as thrilled as you are to welcome a newcomer.)
- Do not interact with other dogs outside of your home until your veterinarian says so. Most new puppies still need their shots!
- Know the rules (eating, sleeping arrangements, etc.) before you bring your puppy home. Don't make them up as you go along. Then gently but firmly enforce them to your new puppy.
- Keep to the mealtime schedule and food your veterinarian has recommended.
- Frequent potty breaks, every twenty to forty-five minutes and after eating are usual for a new pup. When it is time pick him up and take him to the designated outdoor potty area. When he eliminates reward him with a tiny, yummy treat immediately.
- Play! Pups need mental and physical exercise, and it creates a fun time for both of you. Play with toys and run with him in the yard—exercise is good for you too. Remember, a tired pup is a good pup.
- A pup can sleep between sixteen and eighteen hours a day. Naps are necessary to help him grow. Put his crate in a quiet place. Set a bedtime and help him get used to it.

You both can do this!

Dylan's Dog Squad

Dear Dylan's Dog Squad,

My problem is keeping my new puppy out of mischief. I bought a book written for first-time dog owners and followed its recommendations for puppy proofing my home. I installed child gates and child proof locks, but Alfie is very creative. I've had to unplug all wires and keep them out of reach because he prefers them to the chew toys. A tiny scrap of paper found on the floor is gobbled up in an instant. A loose thread on a sweater I'm wearing becomes a game of tug. I'm also afraid this playfulness isn't a phase but a permanent part of his personality.

I waited until Alfie was ten weeks old before I adopted him. We've been together almost two weeks. That would make him three months old. Isn't that enough time for this puppy phase to be over?

Advice, please.

Zach

Dear Zach,

A good time is the only time Alfie is concerned about. Puppies, in fact, have little concept of time. Alfie's concept of time revolves around routine and daily patterns.

Dogs can't understand time in the abstract of hours, minutes, or days. For you two weeks may be long enough to learn the rules of the house but to Alfie, he's just getting started. Besides, he's having a blast.

We think Alfie will get the hang of this soon.

Dylan's Dog Squad

Dear Dylan's Dog Squad,

Our neighbor passed away suddenly. Unfortunately, her grown children were unable to take her five-month-old Dachshund puppies. We've never had dogs before, never thought about having dogs before but the pups are brother and sister. We couldn't let them go to a shelter. They are now ours and we love them. What is the best age to neuter or spay a puppy?

Lillian and Ramon

Dear Lillian and Ramon,

We love happy endings! We also love to give advice on dogs and dog training. But when it comes to medical advice your veterinarian is the expert and the one you should trust.

If you are unable to use your neighbor's veterinarian, ask your dog friends who their vets are. Personal recommendations are always best, and dog people love to share. Luckily, in today's world it's easy to check for veterinary clinic ratings just as you would for a new doctor for yourself.

Then visit the clinic for a consultation. Is it clean? While you are waiting to be seen talk to the other dog owners. What do they say? Take the time to talk to the staff and veterinarian. Do they express interest/concern for your pups? First impressions are usually the ones that count.

Dylan's Dog Squad

DEAR DYLAN'S DOG SQUAD

DEAR DYLAN'S DOG SQUAD,

I'm adopting a medium sized, eight-month-old male dog from a volunteer dog organization. Since his breed is uncertain, I'm going to call him Alias. The organization is taking care of neutering and shots. They explained the advantages of crate training and it seems to be a good idea. I'm just not sure how to start. Any hints?

Shelley

DEAR SHELLEY,

We love the name Alias! Very clever.

Crate training can provide a haven of safety and comfort for Alias. Puppies love to explore but you may not want him to have full reign of your home immediately, especially if he isn't potty trained. Also, he could fall down the stairs or discover so many tempting things to nibble on.

Tips to Make Both of You Happy, Part 1

- Choose a collapsible crate. This will come in handy when traveling with Alias.
- Set the crate up in your bedroom. He will be comforted to know you are near at night. This will ease separation anxiety which can come after leaving a familiar place. When the crate isn't in use make sure the door is open and secured. You don't want Alias to get trapped inside or frightened if it bangs shut.
- Make sure the crate is big enough for him to stand up, turn around, stretch out on his side, and have a toy with him. If the crate is too large, he may misunderstand and think he can eliminate in the corner.
- Crates should never be used for punishment.

- Use treats to encourage Alias to go into the crate on his own.
- Don't leave him in there too long. Pups under six months of age shouldn't stay in the crate for more than three hours at a time. This can cause depression and anxiety.
- Make sure Alias has frequent potty breaks. He's still a puppy!
- The crate should have a comfortable firm bed, and the door should be left open when you are home. Alias will soon regard it as his own doggie clubhouse and will come and go on his own.

Tips to Make Both of You Happy, Part 2

- Crate training can take days or weeks. *Be patient!*
- Set the crate up in your bedroom and leave the door open. Let Alias sniff it and wander in and out. Some dogs will hop in and settle down. Yay! If he does praise him and give him a yummy treat.
- If Alias has no interest in the crate, use a happy voice to bring him over to it. (No baby talk. Dogs hate hearing it as much as humans do.) Make sure the door is open and secured so it doesn't close on its own.
- Sit down in front of Alias and near the crate. Show him a tiny treat. (Yummy treats are always the best.) Then create a treat trail leading up to the crate. Put one treat inside the crate.
- If he goes in praise him and give him another treat.
- If Alias eats all the treats and stares back at you, don't force him into the crate.
- Stay sitting near the crate. This time show him the treat and gently toss it inside the crate.

- Do this a few times.
- If Alias refuses to enter, try putting the treat just inside the crate, close to the crate door. If Alias eats the treat but does not go in, try again with the next treat farther back in the crate. Each time move the treat farther and farther back.
- After Alias successfully goes into the crate a few times, you are ready to take the next step. At mealtime put his dish inside the crate. (Be sure to put a cloth under his dish. Pups are sloppy eaters, and this will save you from washing the pillow.)
- When Alias goes inside to eat, close the door and sit outside until he is finished. Praise him and immediately open the door.
- Gradually let Alias stay in his crate for up to ten minutes after he has finished eating. Always stay nearby. Then praise him and release him. Remember to take him to go potty!

Tips to Make Both of You Happy, Part 3

- After Alias becomes comfortable eating his meals in his crate you can confine him for short times while you are home.
- Call him over to the crate using a command, such as "Crate." Encourage him to enter the crate by gesturing inside the crate with a treat in your hand.
- When Alias enters, praise him, give him the treat, and close the door. Sit quietly near the crate for five or ten minutes and then go into another room for a few minutes. When you return sit quietly again for a few minutes then let him out.

- Repeat this several times a day, increasing the length of time you leave him in the crate and stay out of sight. (Don't leave him too long! He's still a puppy.)
- Once Alias will stay quietly in his crate for thirty minutes with you out of sight, you can try letting hm sleep there at night. Then for short times when you are away from home.
- This may take several days or weeks. *Be patient.*
- When you return don't greet Alias in an exaggerated excited manner. Do so calmly. Praise Alias and give him a treat.
- Continue to crate him for short periods of time when you are at home so he doesn't associate crating with being left alone.

If Alias whines while in the crate at night, he might have to go outside to eliminate. Never punish for whining. Instead, use the command for going potty and take him outside. Once he eliminates bring him back to his crate. If the whining persists, ignore Alias. He is testing you. Again, never punish for whining.

Lastly, separation anxiety can't be solved with crate training. If that is the case, instead consult a professional animal behavior specialist and get Alias the help he needs.

Dylan's Dog Squad

Dear Dylan's Dog Squad,

Our four-month-old Pug, Brinkley, is a sociable little guy. We entertain often and he gets along with everyone he meets. New situations don't seem to bother him.

For some reason when our ten-month-old granddaughter Natalie comes to visit, Brinkley becomes a different dog. His nose quivers and he backs away from her. As soon as Brinkley can he finds somewhere else to be. My husband and I do not understand this behavior. Natalie and Brinkley are not left together unsupervised, and Natalie is allowed to pet Brinkley only with our help. Brinkley doesn't behave aggressively toward her, and he doesn't misbehave, so we don't think he's jealous. What are your thoughts?

Candace

Dear Candace,

Babies are adorable and cute and wonderful and... well, smelly. Especially a ten-month-old in diapers.

A dog's sense of smell is ten thousand to one hundred thousand times better than a human's. The reason is pretty simple: For every scent receptor a human has, a dog has about fifty. A fun fact is dogs with shorter noses such as Pugs are typically better at following a scent than other dogs.

The good news is, they are both young and can grow up together. Eventually Natalie will be out of diapers. Our guess is that soon you won't be able to separate them.

Dylan's Dog Squad

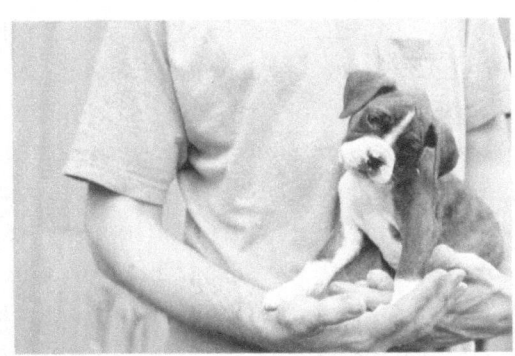

Dear Dylan's Dog Squad,

I'm getting a Boxer pup in two weeks. I've puppy proofed my house, lined up a vet visit, have all the supplies he will need, and Puppy Class starts in three weeks. I think I'm ready, but I keep hearing people say I need to train him to be a Velcro dog. What's that?

Thanks,
Leo

Dear Leo,

The term Velcro dog can refer to a dog that is clingy, often suffering from separation anxiety. We're offering the following explanation instead.

Velcro dog can also refer to training a dog to follow you or to stay near you. The goal is to teach the pup where it can go rather than let it wander around and get into trouble eating things and doing things it shouldn't. This type of training is especially useful if your dog has a history of bad behavior.

To do this attach a four-foot, lightweight leash to your dog's collar. (Anything longer and you will trip over it.) If you walk across the room, *always* take your dog with you. If you walk from one room to another, *always* take your dog with you. Be consistent. After a few weeks keep the leash on your dog but let it drag on the ground. (Another reason for a short leash.) When you leave the room, your dog should follow you without being told to do so. If not, take him with you until he can successfully follow you on his own.

There are many different training programs—for you and your dog. (That's right. You are being trained too.) Always be patient and kind to your dog. Never yell at him and never use his name with a negative command. Praise and reward with yummy treats.

Good luck with your pup!

Dylan's Dog Squad

Dear Dylan's Dog Squad,

We've never had a puppy or dog before. Now we have Boss a three-pound Yorkie. So far potty training has been an adventure and he's enjoying every minute. We're at our wits end. Friends have suggested pee pads. We're not sure.

Crystal and Tom

Dear Crystal and Tom,

Pee pads are a convenient and lazy way to train your pup. Boss is too young to know the difference between a pee pad and your gorgeous wall-to-wall carpeting. He will get the two confused.

Your vet will likely tell you that potty training for Boss will require patience and time. Simply, he's a little guy and it's a short trip from his mouth to eliminating what he's eaten. This means you will have to take him outside sooner after eating than you would if he were a bigger dog and more frequently. He just can't hold it as long as a bigger dog can. Make sure you have designated a potty place in your yard and take him there. When he eliminates praise him and give him a yummy treat. Soon he will come to realize that is his spot.

Never yell at or punish Boss if he has an accident in the house. Just increase the frequency of your visits to his designated potty place. He'll catch on. Remember, dogs really want to please you.

Dylan's Dog Squad

DEAR DYLAN'S DOG SQUAD,

Training is going very well with Tabitha, our six-month-old Great Dane. Except she refuses to drink from her water bowl. Instead, she prefers to drink from the toilet bowl. We've tried everything to make her stop but before we know it, her head is in the bowl and she's happily gulping down the water. Yeck. What can we do? We've tried everything to make her stop.

Rex and Alma

DEAR REX AND ALMA,

Put down the toilet lid.

Letting Tabitha drink from the toilet bowl is gross. Toilet bowls harbor bacteria such as E. coli and can contain toxic chemicals left over from household cleaners.

Dogs are often attracted to the water in a toilet bowl because the water is cold. Try this. Let Tabitha see you put ice cubes in her water dish and then offer her the dish to drink. If she refuses, dip you finger in the cold water and gently brush your finger over her lips. If she's after cold water, she will get the idea and help herself.

Dylan's Dog Squad

Dear Dylan's Dog Squad,

My brother George and his wife Marlena work from home, don't have a social life, don't have children but do have a Shih Tzu named Mimi. They dress her up in designer outfits, she wears ridiculous booties with peep toes showing off nails with nail polish that match her outfits, she wears hair ribbons and for two years I've heard them talk baby talk to her—nonstop.

I finally snapped and told George to knock it off. My wife was horrified (but I think secretly she was on my side). I suppose I should have said it better but enough is enough.

Geoffrey

Dear Geoffrey,

You left out the best part. What happened next?

Anyway. People talk baby talk to a dog to feel at ease and to bond with them. One view is the dog will find it comforting. Another view is that it's better to use a calm and commanding voice with a dog. We prefer the latter. A gentle, everyday voice is what your dog is used to and will naturally respond to. Plus, it won't annoy the dog or those within hearing.

Dylan's Dog Squad

P.S. As for the nail polish we must add that it's necessary to consult a veterinarian before applying any product to a dog's paws. The paws are sensitive and products can cause irritation.

THREE

WANTING ISN'T GETTING

DEAR FRIENDS,

A dog is man's best friend and you should be his. The bond you create will last a lifetime and bring you both great comfort and joy. Your reasons for getting a dog can be as individual as the kind of dog you want. Beyond the reasons of always wanting a dog for companionship or protection you need to think this through before you act. Every dog deserves a forever home and the commitment you make should be for his lifetime.

It's rare that anyone knows everything there is to know about owning a dog the first time around, but you can give it your best try.

Tips to Make Both of You Happy

- Get a dog when you are ready. Act with knowledge, not on whim.
- Know the rules of your house (eating, sleeping arrangements, etc.) before you bring your dog home. If you make up rules as you go along, there will be no consistency and your dog won't know what you expect or what is acceptable behavior.
- Have a veterinarian and groomer lined up before you bring your dog home. Speak to your dog friends first. Visit a few vets and groomers to get a feel for them. Do an internet search and read their reviews.
- Listen to your veterinarian and adopt a feeding schedule. It's easy to overfeed a dog. They love to eat!
- Adopt a training plan and stick to it. Neither you nor your dog will learn all there is to know right away. Set realistic goals. Victories, whether big or small, will inspire your next level of training.
- Socialize your dog with people and other animals when your veterinarian says it's time. If you are adopting a

puppy, he will need to have all his shots before being exposed to outsiders and other animals.
- Adopt a routine exercise program and stick to it. Dogs and people thrive on consistency. Establish a set time for walks, such as after dinner.
- Prepare for accidents in the house—they happen! Never scold your dog or use a harsh voice or his name in a negative way. They don't understand. Instead use reinforcement and praise.
- Know in advance what to do when "What If ...?" happens. In case of evacuation, you should have an emergency packing list for your family. Include your dog's supplies and medications on the list too. Keep a list of all medications (yours and his) on your cell phone too.
- Remember that it takes love, patience and consistency to be a good dog owner and to have a happy dog.

You both can do this!

Dylan's Dog Squad

Dear Dylan's Dog Squad,

Recently we got our first dog. Maggie is a seven-month-old rescue pup. We want to start basic training but everything we've researched is a bit overwhelming. A friend suggested canine boot camp. Maggie is just settling in, and we don't like the idea of her being away from home for a month. What do you suggest?

Bob and Rhea

Dear Bob and Rhea,

If you ask twenty people about dog training, you'll get twenty different answers.

We're not advocates of canine boot camp. Dog training is an excellent opportunity for you and Maggie to bond but that would be impossible if you and Maggie aren't going through training together. (That's right, you are getting trained too.)

Many local pet stores offer beginning dog training classes. These classes are usually small and taught by one trainer and possibly an assistant. To get a feel for how the trainer teaches, ask if you and Maggie can observe one or two classes. This will allow you to see how the owners and their dogs react to the trainer. Every trainer has their own style. We believe a patient but firm approach is best. Remember that dogs learn faster if they're having a good time. And there is nothing that says Maggie can't have fun while she is learning.

When it comes to making your final decision, trust your instincts on this one.

Dylan's Dog Squad

DEAR DYLAN'S DOG SQUAD

Dear Dylan's Dog Squad,

My dog Ruby has every toy imaginable. I play with her constantly. She gets enough exercise to qualify for Canine Olympics.

But Ruby has the habit of suddenly disappearing. When I do find her, she is chewing on my things. Ruby doesn't play favorites. Nothing is safe from her nimble nibbling. Dirty socks, wet bath towels, books, and computer and cell phone charging cords have all bitten the dust.

Ruby's last snack was a pair of new Jimmy Choo shoes that I skipped lunches for a month to afford.

What do I do?

Help!
Lizzie

Dear Lizzie,

Pick up your stuff.

Even though you don't think Ruby's chewing on your Jimmy Choo shoes is a compliment, it is. Ruby loves you and your possessions have your scent. Also, dogs like to chew because it feels good. Ruby merely wants to have something of yours to chew on because it reminds her of you.

As a dog owner you have many jobs other than feeding, exercising, and caring for your furry friend. One job that is often overlooked is giving Ruby the opportunity to do well. She can't go on a chewing spree if your things aren't available.

Dylan's Dog Squad

Dear Dylan's Dog Squad,

Pork Chop, my Weimaraner, has so much energy she could run marathons. To help her burn off excess energy I take her to the park every day and let her run off leash in the open spaces. Last week Pork Chop was having a really good time until the park ranger caught her running off leash, barking and chasing the ducks. I explained that Pork Chop is a high energy dog, but he cited me anyway. I had to pay twenty-seven hundred bucks and now Pork Chop has a rap sheet. This isn't fair.

Signed,
Joe

Dear Joe,

You're right. When you disregarded the rules it wasn't fair to Pork Chop, the ducks or anyone else at the park.

Dylan's Dog Squad

Dear Dylan's Dog Squad,

My wife and kids let Oscar, our seventy-five-pound Giant Schnauzer, beg food from the table, chase our cat, get on our furniture (including our new leather sofa), dig holes in our yard, jump on visitors, terrorize delivery men, and do whatever he wants. When I try to stop Oscar, my family laughs and tells me to lighten up. I know Oscar's bad behavior isn't good for anyone and certainly not for him. Still, I'm exhausted trying to maintain some order. I don't want to be the alpha dog.

Robert

DEAR ROBERT,

Who does? It's lonely at the top. Being the alpha dog can be like being the strict parent who tells kids to eat their broccoli. Every parent wants to be the fun one.

No one likes a bully—whether it be people (your family) or pets (Oscar). We're assuming you tried talking to your family and got nowhere. No doubt they would be devastated if Oscar failed to obey you on a walk and ran into the street and got hurt—or worse. Try educating them and explaining that people have lost their homes because their dog has bitten or hurt someone. Also, dogs have been quarantined or even euthanized for such bad behavior.

What to do now? Educate yourself and Oscar. Start by enrolling in a basic obedience class. Socialization with other dogs and people will do you both good. Teach Oscar basic skills, such as Sit, Stay/Release, Heel, and Come. (You will find these skills in Chapter Six. Basic American Sign Language and Hand Commands are found in Chapter Seven.) Oscar will recognize you as the alpha dog, the one who keeps him safe and the one he respects.

By creating boundaries for Oscar, you will be the one he counts on and comes to when he is scared, lonely or needs help because he knows he can count on you.

Dylan's Dog Squad

P.S. Your cat will thank you, too.

Dear Dylan's Dog Squad,

I've always wanted a dog but wasn't sure what I was looking for. Then I read the Dylan's Dog Squad series. I'm still amazed at all the things Dylan knows and can do. Please tell me how I can get a dog just like Dylan.

Thank you,
Bree

Dear Bree,

Dylan didn't come to us this way! To illustrate, here's an excerpt from "About Dylan Easter Troy," found at the end of this book.

Dylan was born on Easter in Daejeon, South Korea. His owner bought him from Walmart. At that time, I suggested basic dog training, but his owner didn't think training was important. Dylan immediately destroyed his owner's apartment by chewing his way through electrical coverings, baseboards, and furniture. When Dylan ate the interior of his owner's BMW, his owner decided having a dog was too much work and didn't want him anymore.

Yikes! By the time Dylan was eighteen months old he was a serial chewer and had lost his home and his family. All because his owner didn't bother to train him.

Many local pet stores and local community centers offer individual and group classes for dogs four months and older. Dogs are easy to train because they're highly motivated by food, thrive when they have a sense of purpose and have an innate desire to please their owner.

There is more to training than merely learning the rules. Training classes will allow you and your dog to socialize with other owners and their dogs. You may have had dogs before and have taken them to training but don't expect the same results. Keep in mind this will be a new experience for not only your new dog but for the two of you together. It takes time for an owner and a dog to bond and to effectively work together. There is no shame in repeating the class. It would be a shame if you didn't try.

Dylan's Dog Squad

DEAR DYLAN'S DOG SQUAD,

Indigo my one-hundred-sixty-pound Great Pyrenees loves to ride in my Mustang. This is good because I am a sales rep and Indigo can travel with me every day. I love his company and we are very close.

Indigo rides in the backseat. When we are driving, he likes to go from side-to-side looking out the windows. Maybe he likes scenery? Indigo likes to hang his head over my shoulder and whine. Maybe he likes my driving? He likes to lick the side of my face. Maybe he likes my makeup? He also likes to snuffle my neck. Maybe he's happy? Anyway, by the end of the day I've got dog slobber all over me and everywhere. When we're at home, he will sit when I tell him to, but not when we're driving. Maybe he thinks different rules apply in the car?

Signed,
Hailey

DEAR HAILEY,

"Maybe" nothing. Nobody likes a backseat driver, no matter how happy he is. Invest in a comfortable crash tested harness with a strap that will attach to the seatbelt already installed in your car. It may take a little while for Indigo to get used to being tethered in one place, but it is for the best. Otherwise, if you have to stop suddenly, your happy dog will become a one-hundred-sixty-pound missile. Indigo could end up in the front seat of your vehicle or hitting the windshield, causing him great harm or even death. It's your job to keep both of you safe.

Dylan's Dog Squad

P.S. Give Indigo a treat when you attach him to the seatbelt and tell him good boy. He will be happy to get a treat and won't hold a grudge.

DEAR DYLAN'S DOG SQUAD,

Tara is four years old and six pounds. A great dog, mostly. She knows basic commands but when people come over, she becomes Tara the Terrible and likes to jump on them. Since she is only six pounds, no harm is done, but it isn't nice. Is it too late to teach Tara some manners?

Thanks,
Rob

DEAR ROB,

It's never too late for manners. All dogs learn at different speeds. It's important for you to be patient and consistent.

Most people tend to shriek or turn away when a dog jumps on them. Dogs jump because they want attention. Little dogs luck out because they're cute. If Tara were a bigger dog, the reaction wouldn't be the same. Nor would the consequences.

Practice this with Tara. When she hunches and starts to jump, *slowly and carefully* walk into her. You want this to be a gentle bump into her rather than an assault. This will interrupt her momentum, throwing her and her jump off balance. As you bump into her say, "Off." Do not say, "Down." (Down should be used to tell Tara to lie down.) If you have taught Tara hand commands (see Chapter Seven), say, "Down" and give her the hand command at the same time. Because dogs are highly motivated by food, follow this up with a tiny, yummy treat. Tara will catch on.

Dylan's Dog Squad

DEAR DYLAN'S DOG SQUAD,
We read *Dylan's Dilemma* and *Dylan's Dream* in class. We have dogs and we want to teach them how to sit. Can we?

Love,
Bridgett, Noah, JoJo, and Riley
5th Grade

DEAR BRIDGETT, NOAH, JOJO, AND RILEY,
Of course you can! Skills are good for your dog to learn because they will make him a good canine citizen and will also help you to keep him safe.

Let's get started.

1. Put a small treat in your right hand.
2. Get your dog's attention by bringing the treat close to his face.
3. Let him sniff and nibble at the treat. (Watch your fingers. Dog teeth are sharp.)
4. Then slowly bring the treat over his head.

5. As your finger moves out of his line of vision he will naturally back up.
6. When his rump hits the ground, point and say "Sit." Give him the treat and tell him he is a great dog.
7. Practice this ten to fifteen times but don't wear him out. Practice should be for short periods of time. Take a break and practice again later in the day. Learning should be fun for both of you.

Dylan's Dog Squad

P.S. Don't forget the yummy treats!

DEAR DYLAN'S DOG SQUAD,

Walking my dog Ripley is a death-defying experience. No matter what I do, what I try, he is determined to cut in front of me, zip toward and into every bush and greet any and all as if he's been parted from human company for a hundred years. My one and only wish is that Ripley will learn to walk on a leash without yanking my arm out of its socket. Is this possible? I've spent a fortune on trainers, but he doesn't get it. Or doesn't want to.

Sincerely,
Noah

P.S. He's three years old and *big*.

DEAR DYLAN'S DOG SQUAD

Dear Noah,

It's never too late to try.

1. We suggest you put tiny, yummy treats in a small plastic bag and put them in a fanny pack that you wear around your waist. This keeps your hands free to hold the leash, etc.
2. Even though Ripley is big, start training in a small room, such as a bedroom.
3. Clip Ripley's leash to his collar and place him on your left side. When he is sitting, note where his nose comes to on your leg. If Ripley knows Stay, tell him now. This is the Heel position.
4. Hold Ripley's leash in your left hand.
5. Praise Ripley and give him a treat, making sure to offer the treat at nose level. Do this three or four times, pausing briefly in between, until he gets used to being fed in the Heel position. When you are not giving Ripley a treat, keep your hand at waist level.
6. Take a small step forward. Don't drag him or scold him if he does not follow.
7. Try it again. As soon as Ripley takes a step forward, praise him and give him a treat at nose level.
8. Repeat this until Ripley moves forward with you every time you take a small step.
9. Slowly increase the length of your steps until you reach your normal walking step.
10. You're ready to add the command. As you are taking your first step, say "Heel." When Ripley follows, stop and give him a treat. Make sure you praise him. This is a big accomplishment!
11. Practice this until you can start to take two or three steps before giving Ripley a treat. If he refuses to follow, go back to giving more treats more frequently.

12. When Ripley will heel with less frequent treats, move to a larger room. Start with step 3 and repeat the exercise. If this goes well, (again) start to reduce the number of treats you give to Ripley.
13. Eventually you will be ready for the backyard. Start with step 3 and continue until Ripley is comfortable with Heel.
14. The neighborhood walk is next. Go slowly, starting with step 3. Praise often and don't forget the treats.
15. Keep in mind the world is an exciting happy place for Ripley. Keep him at Heel for five minutes at a time. Then give him a break by letting him sniff and look at what he wants. When you are ready to walk, put him in Heel and begin.

Tips to Make Both of You Happy

- Keep training sessions short, no more than five minutes.
- Make sure the treats are very small and very yummy.
- The purpose of Heel is to keep your dog close to you and safe. Walks are supposed to be fun and mentally stimulating for Ripley. During a walk let Ripley set the pace. This is his time to be a dog.

Dylan's Dog Squad

Dear Dylan's Dog Squad,

Thanks for coming to our class. We want to know if every dog can take the AKC Canine Good Citizen Test or does he have to be an American Cocker Spaniel like Dylan? Gator is a Doberman and Enzo is a Dalmatian. Is the test hard? Gator and Enzo are smart. We think it would be really cool if they got a patch to wear on a vest like Dylan does.

Thanks,
Adam and Henry, 5th Grade
O'Hara Intermediate School

Dear Adam and Henry,

Our pleasure! We love school visits.

Training for the American Kennel Club (AKC) Canine Good Citizen Test is a wonderful way for you to bond with your dogs. Any dog can take the test and at any age. You can find out where the test is being offered by contacting your local pet stores or dog training facilities. Once you sign up for the training you will be given information. The American Kennel Club Canine Good Citizen Test actually consists of ten smaller tests. Each tests a different skill, but this is basically what you need to know.

AKC Canine Good Citizen Test Summary

- **Test 1:** Accepting a friendly stranger. This test demonstrates that a dog will allow a friendly stranger to approach and speak to its handler. While the handler and the stranger are engaged in conversation and ignoring the dog, the dog must remain calm and show no resentment or shy away.
- **Test 2:** Sitting politely for petting. This test demonstrates that the dog will allow a friendly stranger to pet it while the dog is sitting by the handler's side. During this test the evaluator will pet the dog on its head and body. The dog must show no sign of resentment or shy away.
- **Test 3.** Appearance and grooming. This tests both the dog and its handler. The handler provides a comb and brush. The evaluator will gently comb or brush the dog, examine its ears and gently pick up each front paw. The dog demonstrates acceptance of being groomed, handled and examined by a vet, a friendly stranger or a groomer. The evaluator will also examine the dog to determine if it is healthy and clean. During this test the handler may talk to the dog and give it praise.
- **Test 4.** Out for a walk (on a loose leash). This test demonstrates the handler is in control of the dog. The dog is allowed to be on either the left or right side of the handler. The dog need not be perfectly aligned with the handler or stop when the handler stops but it needs to demonstrate that the handler is in control. The handler may be given an exact course to follow, or the evaluator may give directions as the test progresses. There should be a left and right turn and at least one stop in between as well as one turn at the

end. The handler may talk and praise the dog along the way.
- **Test 5.** Walking through a crowd. This test demonstrates that the dog is comfortable and under control in public places and moves about politely. The handler may praise and encourage throughout the test, but the dog must not jump on people or pull/tug on the leash.
- **Test 6.** Sit and Down on command and Stay in place. To demonstrate the dog has command of these skills the handler will use a twenty-foot leash. The dog must do Sit *and* Down on command. The handler will choose which position to leave the dog in Stay. The handler may touch the dog to offer gentle guidance but must not force the dog into position. When instructed by the evaluator the handler will walk the length of the leash, turn and return to the dog at a natural pace. The dog may change position but must stay in the place it was left until the evaluator gives the handler the command to release the dog.
- **Test 7.** Coming when called. This test demonstrates that the dog will come when called by its handler. The handler will walk ten feet from the dog, turn to face the dog and then call the dog. The handler may give encouragement to the dog to get him to come.
- **Test 8.** Reaction to another dog. This test demonstrates that the dog can behave politely around other dogs. Two handlers and their dogs will approach each other from a distance of about twenty feet, stop, shake hands and make polite conversation before continuing on about ten feet. During this exchange the dogs may show only a casual interest in each other and no interest in the other handler.
- **Test 9.** Reaction to a distraction. This test demonstrates that the dog is confidant when encountering everyday

distractions and situations. The evaluator will present two distractions such as dropping a heavy object or having a person go by on a skateboard. The dog may show natural interest but should not be startled, try to run away or bark. The handler may encourage and praise during this exercise.

- **Test 10.** Supervised separation. This test demonstrates that a dog may be left with a trusted stranger and still maintain training and good manners. Evaluator will approach the handler, ask to watch the dog, then take hold of the dog's leash. The handler will go out of sight for three minutes. During this time the dog doesn't have to remain in Stay position, but it can't bark, whine or appear nervous. The evaluator may briefly talk to the dog.

This may seem like a lot to learn but Gator and Enzo only have to learn one skill at a time. Before long they will know all ten and be ready to take the test. Remember training is not a race and all dog training requires patience. Instead of worrying about how much there is to learn, think about the fun you will have with your dogs while learning. Teaching them skills that will keep them safe and make them polite canine citizens will make you responsible owners.

Let us know when you pass the test. We're rooting for you!

Dylan's Dog Squad

DEAR DYLAN'S DOG SQUAD

Dear Dylan's Dog Squad,

Panda, my English Sheepdog, really loves his crate. The door is always open and many times I have found him inside, curled up on his pillow. At night he's a good little sleeper and can sleep ten hours straight. Unfortunately, I got up in the middle of the night and tripped over him in the dark. I'm guessing he chose to sleep outside his crate because our nights have gotten warmer. Thankfully, Panda was not hurt.

I feel terrible about what happened, and I've now installed nightlights, so I don't make the same mistake again. My question is, how do I apologize to Panda if I do something wrong? We have a great relationship, and I don't want anything to come between us.

Sincerely,
Nathan

Dear Nathan,

Accidents can happen so quickly. That's why they're called accidents. We're going to borrow from Justice Oliver Wendell Holmes when he remarked that "even a dog distinguishes between being stumbled over and being kicked" (1881). We have a feeling that Panda understands it was an accident and has forgiven you.

If you find yourself in the doghouse with Panda again, don't shout or raise your voice. (This can happen if you are nervous or upset.) Give him a gentle pat on the back. Dogs recognize this as a positive gesture, and it will go a long way toward forgiveness.

Dylan's Dog Squad

FOUR

ROAD TRIP!

Dear Friends,

Summer means road trips and being outside! To make sure your best friend stays cool, comfy, and safe during hot months, here are our tips for you.

🐾 Pawsome Tips Just for You

- **Keep 'em Hydrated:** Fresh, cool water is a must! Add some ice cubes to his bowl for an extra refreshing treat. Your dog will love it!
- **Shady Business:** Make sure there's plenty of shade for your dog to lounge in when outside. Whether it's under a tree or a cozy umbrella, he'll appreciate the break from the sun.
- **Paw Protection:** Hot pavement? No thanks. Walk your dog early in the morning or late in the evening when the ground is cooler and gentler on his paws.
- **Cars Are a No-Go:** Even a few minutes in a hot car can be dangerous. Keep your dog safe by never leaving him unattended in your vehicle.
- **Groom for the Season:** Regular grooming helps keep your dog's coat in top shape. Just be careful not to shave too close. Their fur protects them from sunburn!
- **Cool Treats:** Frozen goodies, anyone? Make some DIY doggie pupsicles with his favorite pet-safe ingredients for a fun, cool-down treat.
- **Easy Does It:** When it comes to playtime, opt for shorter, gentler activities during the hottest parts of the day. Your dog will thank you for the extra chill time.
- **Cooling Gear:** Get him some snazzy cooling mats, vests or bandanas. These nifty items can help your dog beat the heat in style. You could even get one of our Dylan's

DEAR DYLAN'S DOG SQUAD

Dog Squad bandanas. Just send an email to Kathleen@kathleentroy.com

Keep an eye out for any signs of overheating, like heavy panting or drooling, and move your dog to a cooler spot if needed.

We've also included our two favorite DIY doggie pupsicle treat recipes. A little TLC goes a long way in making his summer safe and fun.

Happy trails,
Dylan's Dog Squad

DIY Blueberry Doggie Pupsicle Treats

You will need:

- Baking silicone mold or ice cube trays
- Recommended: baking sheet
- 2 cup measuring cup
- Blender or food processor
- Unsweetened blueberries (or substitute carrots or apples, etc.)
- Plain nonfat yogurt
- Water

INSTRUCTIONS:

1. Whisk together 4 ounces of yogurt and 4 ounces of water. Add more yogurt and reduce the water if your dog prefers a creamier treat.
2. Pour into baking mold/ice cube tray. Leave ample room for the blueberries.
3. Add blueberries to each well until mold is almost filled. The pupsicle will expand as it freezes.

HINTS/TIPS:

1. Clear space in your freezer for your pupsicles to set evenly.
2. If you use a silicone mold place it on a baking sheet BEFORE you fill it. Otherwise, the mold will shift and spill as you put it in the freezer.

DEAR DYLAN'S DOG SQUAD

DIY Peanut Butter Doggie Pupsicle Treats

You will need:

- Baking silicone mold or ice cube trays
- Recommended: baking sheet
- 2 cup measuring cup
- Blender or food processor
- Peanut butter (**IMPORTANT**: *Check the ingredients on the label. Look for no sugar and definitely no xylitol. Xylitol is an artificial sweetener and is poisonous for dogs.*)
- Plain nonfat yogurt
- Water

Instructions:

1. Put 4 ounces of peanut butter in your measuring cup. You needn't be exact.
2. Add 3 ounces of water and 2 ounces of yogurt to the peanut butter. You should have about 9 ounces total.
3. If it doesn't blend add a *little* more water until you reach a pourable consistency.
4. Pour into your molds. Remember these are peanut butter pupsicles so they may be a bit sloppy. No matter--your pup is not a critical audience.

Dear Dylan's Dog Squad,

Every summer our family visits a national park, and we look forward to these road trips. Two months ago, we got Benny, our first dog. At first, we thought we should leave Benny with a sitter, but we all voted no on that. After all Benny is family and he should come, too. Then we were thinking we should postpone our family road trip until we've had Benny longer, but no one liked that idea either. The good news is Benny likes riding in the car and has his own car seat and crash-tested harness. There must be a checklist of what to do when traveling with a dog. Any ideas?

Thanks,
O'Dell Family

Dear O'Dell Family,

What a fun idea. We've got some tips to make this a safe and happy experience.

Tips to Make Both of You Happy

- Put Benny's medical records on your cell phone and put copies in your car.
- Having current contact information, including your cell phone number, on Benny's collar is a must. So is having Benny microchipped if you haven't done so already. This is important in case he should lose his collar. A microchip will help get him back to you quicker.
- Research the rules of the national park you are visiting. Not all welcome dogs.
- Camping or hotel stay? Contact your proposed destination to learn their rules about pets and then decide.

- Along with Benny's bowls, brush, food, yummy treats, vitamins/medication, and shampoo and conditioner (he will get dirty), pack a collapsible crate. The crate is especially necessary if you are planning a hotel stay.
- Scope out dog parks along the way. Road trips start fun but can become monotonous from Benny's point of view.
- On the day of your trip take Benny for a long walk or have a fast game of fetch. If he's tired, he will relax in the car and enjoy a world class snooze.
- Take plenty of walkabout breaks and potty breaks. Benny's first road trip is exciting for him so know that he may need to go potty more frequently. Breaks should be every two to four hours, allowing fifteen to twenty minutes each.
- Be respectful of your environment and pick up after Benny.
- Even though Benny likes riding in the car it's not recommended to feed him prior to a long road trip. Excitement can cause stomach upset. Small, yummy treats along the way are okay. For water, give him small amounts frequently. Have a towel handy just in case.
- Have small, favorite toys in Benny's car seat.
- Pack a first aid kit—for Benny and your family.
- **Never Leave Benny in a Car Unattended.** Eighty degrees is a nice day—unless you are a dog left inside a car. After just twenty minutes, the temperature can rise to almost 110°. After forty minutes, the temperature can reach 118°, and after an hour it can be 123°.

Have a wonderful trip! Send us pictures.

Dylan's Dog Squad

DEAR DYLAN'S DOG SQUAD,

Molly, my Irish Setter, likes to hang her head out the window. Should I let her? I'm afraid she will fall out.

Thank you,
Tim

DEAR TIM,

You should be afraid. Even big dogs have been known to fall out of partially rolled down windows.

When a window is open Molly could not only sustain damage to her ears and eyes from dust and debris, but she could also get hit by flying debris. There's a reason why our cars have windshields. They protect us from dirt, dust, insects, rocks, and other objects that might be in the air. When you are traveling sixty miles per hour even a small rock kicked up by cars in front of you can cause significant damage. Please note that in some states it is actually illegal to let your dog hang its head out the window.

Watching outside activity may be interesting and stimulating for Molly but you need to be careful. Just because Molly is holding still doesn't mean she is relaxed.

Lower the windows no more than three inches, and if it's hot, keep the air conditioner on.

Dylan's Dog Squad

DEAR DYLAN'S DOG SQUAD,

I'm a wine distributor and drive every day for my job. When I got Joey, my Maltese, I took her for a ride, and it went well. She especially liked it when we ended our day by going to the dog park.

The next day she raced me to the car and spun around in a circle until I put her inside. I was happy to have her company. To pass the time, I like to sing in the car. I was thrilled the first time Joey joined in. After a year of hearing her off tune ear-piercing whine and howling nonstop in the car, I'm no longer thrilled.

I tried leaving her home, thinking I misunderstood her. That didn't work either. When I came home, she ignored me and even refused treats.

Joey seems to be upset no matter what I do.

Willa

DEAR WILLA,

Dogs cry or whine when they are excited. If Joey thinks you are going somewhere fun like the park, she may whine in anticipation. If possible, try varying your routine. The less predictable you are the harder it will be for her to figure out the destination.

Dylan's Dog Squad

Dear Dylan's Dog Squad,

Whiskers is a good dog, and she likes to ride in the car. We're going to visit my sister in Colorado in a few weeks. The trip will only take two days, but Whiskers has never ridden in the car that long. I've talked to friends. They have suggested different medications they give their dogs to relax in the car. It seems a pretty good idea. What do you think?

Helena

Dear Helena,

Would you let friends prescribe medication for you?

Your family veterinarian is always the expert when it comes to Whiskers. He knows Whiskers, what kind of dog she is, how much she weighs, etc. If appropriate he will prescribe a medication.

Have fun!

Dylan's Dog Squad

DEAR DYLAN'S DOG SQUAD

Dear Dylan's Dog Squad,

My parents live on a ranch in Montana and recently got the entire family together for a reunion. Tulip, my American Bulldog, had the time of her life. For a solid week she chased after kids, went on trail rides, rode on hay wagons, went to barbecues and sat around the campfire listening to ghost stories. At night she slept like a rock.

When it was time, we said our goodbyes and started driving back to Arizona. It had been a fun week, but I was beat. All I wanted to do was go home and sleep.

Tulip started howling, barking and whining before we even got off the ranch. She's never acted like that before. It got so bad I called our veterinarian. She said it wasn't unusual for dogs to experience overstimulation and then feel a letdown when it was over. She assured me it wasn't serious and that it would pass. She also recommended a mild medication to ease Tulip's distress. I took her advice, Tulip took the medication, and she was better. Even so, it was a long trip home.

Maybe road trips aren't such a good idea for Tulip. I don't like the idea of her always being on medication.

Scott

Dear Scott,

Family reunions are fun! If we were Tulip, we would want to stay on the ranch too.

Now that you are aware of what triggers this response in Tulip, consult your veterinarian before your next road trip to Montana. She may recommend having on hand "just in case" medication. Better yet, invite your family to visit you.

Dylan's Dog Squad

Dear Dylan's Dog Squad,

We just bought a cabin in upstate New York and will be spending our first Christmas in the snow. Lacey, our Afghan Hound, is going with us. We've bought her a waterproof coat and booties, but she hates the booties. At first, she bit them and then she tried to gnaw them off. Now she stands still and refuses to move. We tried coaxing her with treats but that didn't work.

In order for us to get to our cabin, we will be traveling through states with snow. We will be making rest stops along the way and Lacey will need to get out of the car to go potty. We've read that snow can cause injuries to her paw pads and we don't want that. Any ideas?

Thank you,
Alec and Nora

Dear Alec and Nora,

Put knee socks on Lacey. They may not be as glamorous as booties, but they will do the job. Also, because the knee socks will cover most of Lacey's long legs the snow will not cling to her fur and cause matting. To ensure a snug but not too tight fit (you don't want them to bag and have Lacey trip) secure the knee socks with scrunchies.

Dylan's Dog Squad

DEAR DYLAN'S DOG SQUAD

DEAR DYLAN'S DOG SQUAD,

I'm taking Diesel, my two-year-old Husky, on his first road trip. He likes riding in the car and often we'll spend a whole day running errands. It's going to be just us guys living the good life, going from the Pacific Ocean to the Atlantic Ocean. Along the way we'll do a little camping but other than that, no real plans.

My girlfriend thinks having no plans is a bad idea. She keeps saying the trip will be too long for Diesel. I think she's just jealous because I'm taking Diesel and not her.

Tommy

DEAR TOMMY,

Your girlfriend isn't jealous, she's right. Road trips with Diesel need planning. We've put together some ideas.

Tips to Make Both of You Happy

- Make sure Diesel is healthy. Visit your veterinarian at least thirty days prior to your trip. Get a copy of Diesel's vaccinations, make sure he is microchipped, and have an adequate supply of all medications as well as preventative medication for fleas, ticks, and heartworm. Keep a copy of his medical info on your phone, too.
- Book pet-friendly accommodations in advance. Be aware of pet fees and policies. Some hotels, vacation spots, and campgrounds have dog restrictions or dog size restrictions.
- Ask your vet to recommend travel insurance and get it. The unexpected does happen.
- Pack a crash-tested harness, collapsible carrier or crate, collapsible dog dishes, plenty of food and water, two

leashes (one may get lost), his bed, towels (in case he gets sick in the car), pet wipes, poop bags, and a doggy life vest if you will be near/on the water. Bring his favorite chew toys and yummy treats to keep him busy and happy.

- **Important:** Do not skip Diesel's long walk or exercise before you leave. It's best to have him tired out and ready for a world class snooze when you take off. A light meal several hours prior to leaving is okay but stick to treats in the car or a very light meal. Preventing dehydration is as necessary for Diesel as it is for you. Stop for frequent water breaks.
- **Equally important:** Make sure Diesel is restrained while he is riding in the car. (In some states, it is the law.) A carrier is safest–this is where his collapsible crate comes in handy. The carrier needs to be secured with a harness or seatbelt. Should you opt for a dog bed instead, Diesel will need a crash-tested harness that is secured with the seatbelt. Never secure his collar to the seatbelt. In case of an accident, Diesel can become a flying object and suffer strangulation or choking.
- Road trips should be fun! Make this a fun time for Diesel and stop for frequent breaks. It will be good for both of you to run around or go for a long walk. Dogs can become bored during a road trip. If he starts to whine, it's time to take a break.
- Do something new. Stop at an outdoor café, go kayaking, find a new dog park, have a picnic dinner on a cliff, and watch the sun go down.
- Always leave your travel spot better than you found it.

Send pictures!
Dylan's Dog Squad

FIVE

OH WOW! CHOW!

DEAR FRIENDS,

A dog may not want to eat for many reasons. He isn't hungry or it's too hot. He's too excited or the humans overdid it with treats. The reasons may be more serious such as he is recovering from surgery, mourning a death, stress, aging or illness. One skipped meal isn't much to worry about. Dogs can go for a few days without eating as long as they are drinking water. But if your furry friend continues to refuse food, please contact your veterinarian. She may recommend the following methods to inspire your dog to eat.

- Give your dog a treat. Sure, it's bribery but it may help you decide if the situation is more serious. Give your dog a *little* something that he considers special. Just don't overdo it.
- Change food brands. Dogs just like people get tired of the same old, same old.
- Heat up your dog's food. It may sound crazy, but hey, we all know pizza tastes different cold out of the refrigerator compared to hot out of the box.
- Add broth to your dog's food. If your dog isn't used to this, it may do the trick. (Slightly warm broth is yummier.) Low sodium broth is best.
- Hand feed your dog. Who doesn't like a little extra TLC when they are under the weather? Besides your dog will gain comfort from you being with him.
- Read the instructions on his medications. Dog meds like people meds can cause loss of appetite.

If your dog still avoids food and exhibits any of these symptoms, *definitely* contact your veterinarian as soon as possible.

- Vomiting
- Lethargy
- Weight Loss
- Diarrhea
- Gagging, wheezing or coughing

A dog may be man's best friend. This is the time when you can be your dog's best friend.

Dylan's Dog Squad

Dear Dylan's Dog Squad,

I didn't want the hassle of training a puppy. So, I got Skipper because he's an older dog and already trained. My sister was over yesterday and told me I shouldn't leave Skipper's food down all day. It seems like a good idea to me. Then Skipper can eat when he's hungry and it's one less thing for me to do. What do you think?

John

Dear John,

The first tip-off that a dog is not feeling well is when he is off his food. Allowing Skipper to self-feed means you are not aware of when he is eating, how often he is eating, or how much.

Listen to your sister: feed Skipper at scheduled mealtimes.

Dylan's Dog Squad

Dear Dylan's Dog Squad,

My friend just sent me a video of her German Shepherd, Apollo, after he'd taken down her son's Christmas stocking from the mantle.

In the video Apollo was having a grand time holding a large peppermint stick between his front paws and chewing on it. On the floor was a gigantic chocolate Santa which, thankfully, he hadn't eaten. She thought the video was cute.

I reminded her that since Apollo was the size of a Shetland pony and obviously capable of helping himself to the stocking, she should have seen to it that the stocking was higher up. The amount of sugar in the peppermint stick must be enormous. Not to mention Apollo could have choked on the plastic wrapping. She became very defensive and said I was overreacting.

And now she's not talking to me. Should I apologize?

Veronica

DEAR VERONICA,

No.

Peppermint sticks are not good for dogs.

Sugar isn't good for dogs.

Apollo was very fortunate he hadn't claimed the chocolate Santa. Chocolate can be fatal for dogs to ingest because of the theobromine content which dogs are unable to metabolize effectively. Chocolate can cause vomiting, diarrhea, increased thirst, panting, restlessness, excessive urination and an increased heart rate. In severe cases it can cause cardiac arrhythmias, muscle tremors and seizures.

Please urge your friend to ask her veterinarian for a list of foods that dogs should avoid or are considered to be dangerous or deadly. It is always better to know sooner rather than later.

Dylan's Dog Squad

Dear Dylan's Dog Squad,

Astair our Afghan Hound has long legs and can rest his chin on tables and counters. Last week my son's little league team was at our house for a party, and we ordered four large pizzas. My wife left the opened pizza boxes on the kitchen counter for five minutes while she rounded up the boys. When she returned Astair had dragged his ears across all the pizzas and had eaten most of the toppings along the way. This isn't the first time Astair has done something like this. Last November he snatched the Thanksgiving turkey off the dining room table. This has to stop.

Jerome

Dear Jerome,

In a dog's world any food left out is considered abandoned.

Immediately change your habits. Do not feed Astair from the table or give him treats while you are watching television. Do not let him self-feed. Instead place his food in a dedicated area, the same time every day. (Water may be left out all day.) Save treats for when you take Astair on walks, or to the vet or when he's a good boy. Be sure to praise him when he has done something good.

Dylan's Dog Squad

DEAR DYLAN'S DOG SQUAD

Dear Dylan's Dog Squad,

Albert, my Wheaten Terrier, will eat his wet food for breakfast. After that he begs for treats all day long. He's hard to resist but I do.

You'd think Albert would be half starved by dinner time and eat his kibble. Instead, he turns his nose up and walks away. Recently he learned how to give his bowl a really good push, knocking it over. Then he walked away. I got him a heavier bowl. Now he slides the bowl all over the place, kind of like dog bowl hockey.

I've talked to our vet. He says Albert is healthy and will eat when he gets hungry. I don't like the idea of leaving his kibble down all night, but I don't like the idea of him starving either.

Sincerely,
Gracie

Dear Gracie,

The easy answer is Albert prefers treats to his kibble.

It seems you and your vet have ruled out a medical condition. Consider tricking Albert into eating his dinner by thinking he is getting treats instead. To do this you can't give him any treats during the day.

At night let Albert see you get his kibble from its container and put the kibble in a bowl on a nonskid placemat. (We know. This is really ruining his fun.) If he doesn't eat leave it out for ten minutes and then pick it up. The next night, do the same thing but leave it out for only five minutes before you pick it up. (Since Albert is eating his breakfast, he isn't starving.)

On the third night make a big production out of letting Albert see you get his kibble from a different container (not his normal food container). Tell him to sit and offer him one as a treat. Praise him. If he begs for another give him the sit command again and another treat. Put a *tiny* amount in his bowl. When he finishes, praise him and give him a gentle back rub. Dogs like back rubs and associate it with good behavior. If he asks for more, do not give in.

Gradually increase the amount of "treat kibble" in his bowl until Albert is getting his normal supply. If Albert refuses to be tricked ask your vet to recommend another brand of kibble.

Dylan's Dog Squad

DEAR DYLAN'S DOG SQUAD

Dear Dylan's Dog Squad,

Wendy my toy Pomeranian puppy refuses to eat her food. Before buying it, I researched it thoroughly. It's the most expensive and most nutritious brand on the market. The maker's website showed over one hundred positive testimonials from happy dog owners. She won't even eat it if I offer to hand feed her. I don't understand what the matter is.

Jason

Dear Jason,

She hates it.

Or she may simply prefer a different food. Contact your veterinarian immediately. Dogs love food and when they don't eat there is usually a very good reason. Wendy's non-eating may be a sign of a more important problem but only your veterinarian can confirm or rule that out.

Dylan's Dog Squad

Dear Dylan's Dog Squad,

When I got Garbo, my vet recommended a brand of food and a feeding schedule. The good news is Garbo really likes her puppy chow. The bad news is, she likes it too much. As soon as I set her bowl down her head is in the bowl and the food disappears in a heartbeat. Afterward her stomach rumbles and she is a little gassy. Once she vomited.

I've talked to my vet about this, and he thought she would slow down when she got older. Garbo is almost six months old and faster than ever. She's a Maltese, if that makes a difference.

Celeste

DEAR DYLAN'S DOG SQUAD

Dear Celeste,

Eating too quickly can be a sign of anxiety. Garbo may still be remembering being with her littermates or in a kennel situation and having to scramble for food. Or she just may be a good little eater.

Please talk to your vet again. Garbo is older and she may benefit by a change in diet. Either way, try feeding her by hand.

Tips to Make Both of You Happy

- At mealtime, put Garbo's food in a bowl and sit on the floor and face her. Put her in Sit position. If her food is dry give her one piece at a time. She's still a puppy so watch your fingers! If she jumps up or tries to put her face in her bowl, give her the sit command and wait until she does. Then give her a piece. Wait about five seconds and then give her another piece. This will slow Garbo down giving her a chance to digest her food.
- If Garbo eats wet food, try this. (You may feel silly, but it really works.) Sit on the floor with her bowl of food and face her. Put Garbo in Sit position. Using a fork give her one tiny bite at a time. If she jumps up or tries to go for the food give her the sit command and wait until she does. Then give her another bite.

Dogs with furry faces tend to end up with food in their whiskers and ears. Feeding by hand takes care of that, too!

Dylan's Dog Squad

Dear Dylan's Dog Squad,

My aunt lives on an avocado ranch and her Australian Shepherd has the run of the place. He loves to eat the avocados that have fallen on the ground and always has avocado gunk on his paws and in his fur and ears.

I know avocados are good for people but eating that many avocados can't be good for a dog.

Mathilde

Dear Mathilde,

You're right. It's not.

Before you give any human food to a dog, consult your veterinarian. Large portions of avocados can cause vomiting and diarrhea. Avocados also contain persin, a toxin. Persin is more prevalent in the leaves and skin of the avocado. Since her dog is not likely to be peeling the avocado, this presents two real dangers: Consuming the fruit itself and its seed. Avocados are slippery and it would be very easy for the dog to choke on the seed or have the seed get lodged in its throat.

Dylan's Dog Squad

DEAR DYLAN'S DOG SQUAD

Dear Dylan's Dog Squad,

We were invited to a barbecue at a coworker's house to celebrate Labor Day. We didn't know Clint well but other people from our company were going and it was a chance to mingle. Clint also invited everyone's dogs. It sounded fun.

All was going well until Clint lifted the lid on the barbecue to check the T-bone steaks. Jaws, his Belgian Malinois, came racing out of nowhere. He streaked past Clint, snatched a steak off the grill and kept going.

The other guests cheered and clapped. Jaws took his prize over to the corner of the yard, but chaos soon broke out. The other dogs left their owners and charged over. Jaws was the biggest. He growled, bared his teeth and then wolfed the steak down. We'd never seen anything like it. Clint just laughed. He said that's how Jaws got his name, and he does tricks like that all the time. Besides, Clint assured us, he'd grilled extra steaks.

We didn't think that was the point and said so. We also kept Ginger our, Bichon, on our laps for the remainder of the visit.

Margo and Dave

Dear Margo and Dave,

So many things could have gone wrong here. Grills often flame up when the lid is lifted and Jaws could have been burned. Dogs should always be supervised when chewing on bones, so they don't choke. Also, dogs become territorial over food. Here, Jaws had a steak and the other dogs clearly wanted some. If Jaws wasn't afraid to take a steak off a burning grill, it's doubtful he would have allowed the dogs to take it away from him. Someone's dog could have been hurt or worse.

Clint seems to have little respect for the safety of Jaws or anyone else. You were right to keep Ginger on your lap. Jaws may not recognize the difference between a little dog and a chicken.

Dylan's Dog Squad

DEAR DYLAN'S DOG SQUAD,

Cowboy is about seven years old. We think he is a cattle dog but not really sure. We found him running alongside Highway 46 in Paso Robles about six months ago. He is a really good dog and seems very happy with us.

At mealtime Cowboy will sit and politely wait to be fed. When we put his dish down, he won't eat from the dish. Instead, he will take a small amount out, put it on the floor and then eat it. After he finishes that he will go back for more and do the same thing until he empties the bowl. The first time he did this, we put his food back into his bowl. He took it out again. And again. We have since given up and put his dish on a washable placemat.

We do not have other pets or small children. Other than the occasional TV or music sounds our home is very quiet. Why does he do this?

Thank you,
Geraldo and Yvette

DEAR GERALDO AND YVETTE,

Some dogs develop this habit when they are puppies and are used to competing for food with their littermates. Others learn it later when they are in a kennel or someplace where food isn't plentiful. By taking the food out of his bowl Cowboy is securing a piece just for him.

It is obvious Cowboy has a really good life now. He has good eating habits and doesn't whine or beg for food. Nor does he pounce on his dish immediately when you put it down for him. Those are signs that he is very secure in his new home.

Not to worry. Old habits die hard for dogs, just like they do for people.

Dylan's Dog Squad

P.S. Cowboy is a really great name!

SIX

TRAINING THE HUMANS

Dear Friends,

Training your dog to be a good canine citizen isn't that difficult. All dogs need a purpose, are highly motivated by food and really want the opportunity to please you.

We've included some basic training techniques for Sit, Stay/Release, Heel and Come.

You can choose other words for these skills, but we don't suggest it. The reason is someone may see your dog starting to run across the street. That person is likely to say Stay. Your dog will recognize that skill and stay.

Always remember training is about love, mutual respect, consistency, and *patience*. Dogs learn at different speeds. Some skills may be easier for them to grasp than others.

Lastly, learning is fun and a chance for you and your dog to bond.

Tips to Make Both of You Happy

- It may sound crazy, but you want to first practice skills without your dog. This will allow you to get used to handling the leash, working at a steady pace, and giving tiny, yummy treats. (Not to worry about forgetting this part. Your dog will remind you soon enough.)
- Speaking of treats, wear a fanny pack around your waist. This allows your hands to be free and your dog won't be distracted by seeing the treat. Treats should be very small, something that can be gulped down. Chewing a treat will disrupt the rhythm of the training session.
- Always work in a space free from distractions like other people and noises.
- Never scold your dog or use his name with a negative command.

- Make sure your goals are clear, easy to follow and consistent.
- Did we mention yummy treats?

Following the basic steps for Sit, Stay/Release, Heel and Come, we've included a summary of the American Kennel Club Canine Good Citizen Test, The Responsible Dog Owner's Pledge, and Crate Training Tips.

Dylan's Dog Squad

SIT

SIT IS A BASIC SKILL YOU CAN USE WHEN YOU WANT your dog to calm down, when you don't want him to jump on someone… the reasons are endless.

1. To start, put a small treat in your right hand.
2. Get your dog's attention by bringing the treat close to his face.
3. Let him sniff and nibble at the treat. (Watch your fingers. Puppy teeth are sharp.)
4. Then slowly bring the treat over his head.
5. As your finger moves out of his line of vision he will naturally back up.
6. When his rump hits the ground, point, and say Sit. Give him a treat and tell him he is a great dog.
7. Practice this skill ten to fifteen times but don't wear him out. Do it a few times. Take a break, do something fun and come back to it. Learning should be fun for both of you.
8. When he masters this, try giving him the hand command without the verbal one. (See Chapter Seven.)

Tips to Make Both of You Happy

- Always work in a quiet, familiar place such as your home or backyard.
- This area should be free from distractions like other people, noises, and smells.
- Sit is usually the first skill your dog will learn, so be patient.
- Encourage and praise often. (We all need that!)
- Practice for a few minutes at a time, taking breaks often.
- Be sure to practice every day.

STAY/RELEASE

STAY IS A BASIC SKILL YOU CAN USE MANY TIMES A DAY and in many different situations. You can use it when your dog's paws are muddy and you want him to stop before coming into the house. Or when you've dropped food on the floor in the kitchen. Or simply when you want him to stay in one spot.

1. Start in a quiet and safe place. It's important your dog is able to focus on you.
2. Ask your dog to Sit. (If your dog can't sit on command, it's not likely you can get him to Stay.)
3. Since your dog already knows Sit, do not immediately give a treat. Instead praise him. It's important to be enthusiastic. (Dogs like to be cheered too!) Wait a bit and then give a tiny, yummy treat.
4. When you ask your dog to sit again, wait ten seconds before giving him a treat. Continue this exercise, gradually increasing the time between Sit and giving the treat by three seconds. Then five seconds. Continue until the space between Sit and treat is about fifteen seconds.
5. Practice steps 1-4 until your dog can sit for at least fifteen seconds.
6. Next say Sit and then Stay. Be confidant when you give the command and use a moderate tone. (This is supposed to be fun, and no one likes a bully.) Praise and give a treat.
7. Spend fifteen to thirty minutes a day practicing this command. Translation: Do this for five or ten minutes,

take a break and do it again later in the day for a total of fifteen or thirty minutes.
8. You and your dog are now ready for Release.
9. Start by telling your dog to Sit. After fifteen seconds give the Release command by tossing some treats. Say "Go." (You can add a hand signal, such as lifting your hand.) Be sure to toss the treats a short distance from your dog so he has to get up to get them.
10. Practice step 9, gradually increasing the distance.
11. The combination of Sit, Stay, and Release is a useful everyday skill. For example: You are outside, and a visitor has pulled into your driveway. Give the Sit and Stay command. When it is the right time for your dog to greet the visitor, give the Release command.

Tips to Make Both of You Happy

- Be patient. If you get frustrated, your dog will too. There is always tomorrow.
- The stay command is only meant for *brief* periods of time. Never use the command if you are leaving the house or leaving him unattended.
- Don't forget the yummy treats.

HEEL

Have you ever seen a dog taking a human for a walk? It might be pretty funny unless you are the one on the other end of the leash.

Dogs were originally bred to work on a farm, to go after vermin or to hunt. Modernly dogs without a job to do can easily become bored and get into mischief. Teaching your dog to heel will train him to focus on you and to accept you as the leader. Constantly looking to you is mentally stimulating for a dog and can actually wear him out more than physical exercise.

Two practical reasons for teaching your dog to Heel are safety and good manners. If your dog is startled and slips out of his collar he won't take off or worse, run into the street. Let's say your family reunion is a barbecue. (Every dog's dream.) Food smells fill the air, everywhere people are walking by with food, or you walk by where food has been dropped. Keeping your dog on leash in the Heel position will keep him concentrating on you. This is preferred to keeping him in the Stay position. The Stay position is for short periods of time only. If you leave him in Stay too long, this can cause stress.

1. We suggest you put *tiny, yummy* treats in a small plastic bag and put them in a fanny pack that you wear around your waist. This keeps your hands free to hold the leash, etc.
2. Even if your dog is big, start training in a small room, such as a bedroom.
3. Clip your dog's leash to his collar and place him on your left side. If your dog knows Stay, tell him. When he is sitting, note where his nose comes to on your leg. Your dog is now in the Heel position.
4. Praise him and give him a treat, making sure to offer the treat at nose level. Do this three or four times, pausing briefly in between until he gets used to being fed in the Heel position. When you are not giving a treat, keep your hand at waist level.
5. Take a small step forward. Don't drag him or scold him if he does not follow.
6. Try it again. As soon as your dog takes a step forward, praise him and give him a treat at nose level.
7. Repeat this until he moves forward with you every time you take a small step.
8. Slowly increase the length of your steps until you reach your normal walking step.
9. Create a working zone, allowing your dog to go no farther than eighteen inches ahead of you. (His shoulder should be next to your leg.) He needs to be able to see you in his peripheral vision at all times.
10. You're ready to add the command. As you are taking your first step, say "Heel." When he follows, stop, and give him a treat. Make sure you praise him. This is a big accomplishment!
11. Practice this until you can start to take two or three steps before giving a treat. If he refuses to follow, go back to giving more treats more frequently.

12. When your dog will heel with less frequent treats, move to a larger room. Start with step 3 and repeat the exercise. If this goes well, start to reduce the number of treats you give.
13. Eventually you will be ready for the backyard. Start with step 3 and continue until your dog is comfortable with Heel.
14. The neighborhood walk is next. Go slowly, starting with step 3. Praise often and don't forget the treats.
15. Keep in mind the world is an exciting happy place for a dog. Keep him at Heel for five minutes at a time. Then give him a break by letting him sniff and look at what he wants. When you are ready to walk, put him in Heel and begin.

Tips to Make Both of You Happy

- Keep training sessions short—no more than five minutes.
- Make sure the treats are very small and very yummy.
- The purpose of Heel is to keep your dog safe and close to you when needed. Walks are supposed to be fun and mentally stimulating. During a walk let him set the pace. This is his time to be a dog.

COME

DOGS ARE EASILY DISTRACTED BY OTHER DOGS, BY animals that get into your yard, by a car racing down the street, or by discarded food found on a walk. It's a heart stopping moment when your dog runs off and you can't get him to come back. Teaching your dog the Come skill will give you peace of mind and allow him to enjoy being off leash when it is safe to do so.

You will need:

- A quiet place
- A training leash, ten to forty feet
- Tiny, yummy treats
- Patience
- Enthusiasm

1. Start in a safe quiet spot, such as your backyard or somewhere in your home.
2. Let you dog wander about, sniffing and exploring.
3. After about five minutes, say your dog's name and "Come."
4. Your dog will be watching you. Be enthusiastic!
5. As he starts toward you, praise him, and tell him he is a good boy. Have a happy face and a happy voice. (No one wants to come to a grumpy person.)
6. When he reaches you, give him the treat. Rub his back, ears and add some happy pats. Tell him he did a good job.

Take a break and let him go back to walking around the backyard or room. After a few minutes repeat steps 3-6. Keep your training brief, between fifteen and twenty minutes. Practice every day until he consistently comes to you when called. Then, repeat steps 2-6 but increase your distance.

When your dog is successfully coming when called, go somewhere with distractions such as a dog park. Be alert and be patient. New environments have new smells. If your dog gets distracted, try it again at a later time.

Tips to Make Both of You Happy

- Only begin a training session when you are relaxed, in a good mood and can dedicate the time to your dog.
- Be patient and maintain a good attitude.
- Always use positive reinforcement.
- Never call your dog to punish him, when you are upset or when you are experiencing an upsetting situation.
- Practice Come in a fenced backyard, park, or your home.
- Always carry a leash with you, just in case. Remember, he is a dog first.
- Always microchip your dog and ensure that your most recent contact information is on his ID tag, in case he gets lost.

AKC Canine Good Citizen Test-Summary

- **Test 1:** Accepting a friendly stranger. This test demonstrates that a dog will allow a friendly stranger to approach and speak to its handler. While the handler and the stranger are engaged in conversation and ignoring the dog, the dog must remain calm and show no resentment or shy away.
- **Test 2:** Sitting politely for petting. This test demonstrates that the dog will allow a friendly stranger to pet it while the dog is sitting by the handler's side. During this test the evaluator will pet the dog on its head and body. The dog must show no sign of resentment or shy away.
- **Test 3.** Appearance and grooming. This tests both the dog and its handler. The handler provides a comb and brush. The evaluator will gently comb or brush the dog, examine its ears and gently pick up each front paw. The dog demonstrates acceptance of being groomed, handled and examined by a vet, a friendly stranger or a groomer. The evaluator will also examine the dog to determine if it is healthy and clean. During this test the handler may talk to the dog and give it praise.

- **Test 4.** Out for a walk (on a loose leash). This test demonstrates the handler is in control of the dog. The dog is allowed to be on either the left or right side of the handler. The dog need not be perfectly aligned with the handler or stop when the handler stops but it needs to demonstrate the handler is in control. The handler may be given an exact course to follow, or the evaluator may give directions as the test progresses. There should be a left and right turn and at least one stop in between as well as one turn at the end. The handler may talk and praise the dog along the way.
- **Test 5.** Walking through a crowd. This demonstrates that the dog is comfortable and under control in public places and moves about politely. The handler may praise and encourage throughout the test, but the dog must not jump on people or pull/tug on the leash.
- **Test 6.** Sit and Down on command and Stay in place. To demonstrate that the dog has command of these skills the handler will use a twenty-foot leash. The dog must do Sit *and* Down on command. The handler will choose which position to leave the dog in Stay. The handler may touch the dog to offer gentle guidance but must not force the dog into position. When instructed by the evaluator the handler will walk the length of the leash, turn and then return to the dog at a natural pace. The dog may change position but must stay in the place it was left until the evaluator gives the handler the command to release the dog.

- **Test 7.** Coming when called. The test demonstrates that the dog will come when called by its handler. The handler will walk ten feet from the dog, turn to face the dog and then call the dog. The handler may give encouragement to the dog to get him to come.
- **Test 8.** Reaction to another dog. This demonstrates that the dog can behave politely around other dogs. Two handlers and their dogs will approach each other from a distance of about twenty feet, stop, shake hands and make polite conversation before continuing on about ten feet. During this exchange the dogs may show only a casual interest in each other and no interest in the other handler.
- **Test 9.** Reaction to a distraction. This demonstrates that the dog is confidant when encountering everyday distractions and situations. The evaluator will present two distractions such as dropping a heavy object or having a person go by on a skateboard. The dog may show natural interest but should not be startled, try to run away or bark. The handler may encourage and praise during this exercise.
- **Test 10.** Supervised separation. This test demonstrates that a dog may be left with a trusted stranger and still maintain training and good manners. Evaluator will approach the handler, ask to watch the dog and then take hold of the dog's leash. The handler will go out of sight for three minutes. During this time the dog doesn't have to remain in stay position, but it can't bark, whine or appear nervous. Evaluator may briefly talk to the dog.

Responsible Dog Owner's Pledge

I WILL BE RESPONSIBLE FOR MY DOG'S SAFETY.

I will properly control my dog by providing fencing where appropriate, not letting my dog run loose, and using a leash in public. I will ensure that my dog has some form of identification, which may include collar tags, tattoos, or microchip ID.

CRATE TRAINING

Tips to Make Both of You Happy, Part 1

- To begin, choose a collapsible crate. This will come in handy when traveling.
- Set the crate up in your bedroom. Your dog will be comforted to know you are near. This will ease separation anxiety which can come after leaving a familiar place. When the crate is not in use make sure the door is open and secured. You don't want him to get trapped inside or frightened if it bangs shut.
- Make sure the crate is big enough for him to stand up, turn around, stretch out on his side, and have a toy with him. If the crate is too large, he may misunderstand and think he can eliminate in the corner.
- You will need a comfy firm cushion that fits the crate.
- Crates should never be used for punishment.
- Use treats to encourage him to go into the crate on his own.
- Don't leave him in there too long. Pups under six months of age shouldn't stay in the crate for more than three hours at a time. This can cause depression and anxiety.
- Make sure he has frequent potty breaks. He's a puppy!
- The crate's door should be left open and secured when you are home. Your dog will soon regard it as his own doggie clubhouse and will come and go on his own.

Tips to Make Both of You Happy, Part 2

- Crate training can take days or weeks. *Be patient!* Let your dog sniff it and wander in and out. Some dogs will hop in and settle down. Yay! If he does praise him.
- If your dog has no interest in the crate, use a happy voice to bring him over to it. Make sure the door is open and secured so it doesn't close on its own.
- Sit down in front of him and near the crate. Show him a tiny treat. (Yummy treats are always the best.) Then create a treat trail leading up to the crate. Put one treat inside the crate.
- If he goes in praise him and give him another treat.
- If he eats all the treats and stares back at you, don't force him into the crate.
- Stay sitting near the crate. This time show him the treat and gently toss it inside the crate. Do this a few times.
- If he refuses to enter, try again but put the treat inside, close to the crate door. Then each time move the treat farther and farther back.
- After he successfully goes into the crate a few times, you are ready to take the next step.
- At mealtime put his dish inside the crate. (Be sure to put a cloth under his dish. Dogs are sloppy eaters, and this will save you from washing the pillow.)
- When he goes inside to eat, close the door, and sit outside until he is finished. Praise him and immediately open the door.
- Gradually let him stay in his crate for up to ten minutes after he has finished eating. Always stay nearby. Then praise him and release him.
- Remember to take him to go potty.

Tips to Make Both of You Happy, Part 3

- After your dog becomes comfortable eating his meals in his crate you can confine him for short times while you are home.
- Call him over to the crate, using a command such as "Crate." Encourage him to enter the crate by gesturing inside the crate with a treat in your hand.
- When he enters, praise him, give him the treat, close the door then sit quietly near the crate for five or ten minutes and then go into another room for a few minutes. When you return sit quietly again for a few minutes and then let him out.
- Repeat this several times a day, increasing the length of time you leave him in the crate and out of sight. (Don't leave him too long! He's still a puppy.)
- Once he will stay quietly in his crate for thirty minutes with you out of sight, you can try letting hm sleep there at night. Then for short times when you are away from home. This may take several days or weeks. *Be patient.* When you return don't greet him in an exaggerated excited manner. Do so calmly. (Don't use baby talk. Dogs hate hearing it as much as humans do.) Praise him and give him a treat.
- Continue to crate him for short periods of time when you are at home, so he doesn't associate crating with being left alone.

SEVEN

SHOW TIME!

Dear Friends,

There are so many ways you can bond and communicate with your dog. Using your voice to teach him skills will help him to become a good canine citizen and to keep him safe. By offering an American Sign Language (ASL) sign/hand signal followed by the verbal cue your dog already knows, he will come to understand that they mean the same.

As the leader or alpha dog, your dog will naturally focus on you and will read your body language. This allows him to respond well to signs and hand signals. Also, when a dog ages, he is likely to lose his hearing and ASL signs and hand signals will allow you to continue to communicate with him.

We've included some simple American Sign Language signs and hand commands. Give them a try!

Dylan's Dog Squad

P.S. Not all ASL signs and hand commands must be serious. Our favorite ASL sign is "I love you."

Simple ASL Signs/Hand Commands

- APPLAUSE/YAY: Hold your hands in the air and twist them a couple of times.
- COME: Extend both hands with your index fingers pointing forward and up. Then bend your arms at the elbow and pull your fingers in toward your body.
- (DIRECTIONS) LEFT: Raise your left hand, showing thumb and index finger only. Motion to the left.
- (DIRECTIONS) RIGHT: Raise your right hand, showing your index and third fingers only. Cross your index and third fingers, then point to the right.
- DOWN: Point your index finger down and move your hand in a downward direction.
- GO: "Throw" your index fingers forward. The index fingers trace the air. Throwing the index fingers to the side is popular, too.
- HI: Put your open hand to your forehead then quickly move it away in a salute.
- I DON'T KNOW: Shrug your shoulders.
- I LOVE YOU: Show your little finger, your index finger and your thumb. Tuck the other two fingers into your palm.
- LISTEN: Raise your right hand, curling down your third, fourth and fifth fingers. Point your index finger straight up and point your thumb to your ear.
- NO: Take your first two fingers and tap them against your thumb, resembling a mouth talking.

- (ARE YOU) OKAY?: Point your index finger on your dominant hand toward the person and then quickly withdraw your index finger. With your thumb straight up, make a couple of quick circles.
- QUIET: Bring your index finger to your lips.
- STAY: Move your thumb and little finger forward in a palm-down "Y" shape. The movement is a forward thrust, not a downward slap. You are shoving the knuckles forward and a bit down.
- STOP: Extend your left hand, palm upward. Bring your right hand down to your left hand at a right angle.
- WATCH: Thrust your index and third fingers forward.
- WORK: Close both hands into fists in front of you, then tap your right fist on top of your left fist a couple of times in the wrist area.
- YES: Make a fist and bob it back and forth.

EIGHT

A LITTLE HELP HERE

Dear Friends,

We all need a little help from time to time.

When your dog experiences an illness or an injury always talk to your veterinarian first. They are the expert and have the knowledge necessary to ensure the best treatment for your furry friend. If your dog is aging and starting to slow down, ask your veterinarian for advice. It may simply be time for a different diet or a change in exercise routine. Or it may be time to see a specialist.

Whatever the course of action is, remember that your dog has looked to you for guidance his entire life. Now he needs you more than ever. After all your time together, your dog is an expert at reading your mood. If you are worried or depressed about the changes he is going through, he will pick up on it. He will be worried too, but he won't understand why.

Keep your face positive and your mood enthusiastic. If your dog can no longer go for a long walk, go for shorter walks. Also, consider a dog stroller or a dog bike trailer. Your dog won't wonder what happened. Instead, he will be happy to get out in the world with his friend.

Think of toys and games to mentally stimulate him. Search pet stores for dog toy puzzles. Look for ones that allow you to hide a treat in a compartment. Dogs never lose their sense of smell, and they have to be the most optimistic creatures on earth. If there is any possibility of finding a yummy treat in a dog puzzle, they never tire of trying.

Play a game of Search. Put your dog in Sit or Stay. Let him see you hide and then call Come. If he finds you right away, praise him and give him a treat. Do this two or three times, varying where and how far away you hide. If he seems lost or distracted, try it again but hide closer until he finds you on the first try. The point is to give him some exercise and to boost his confidence. And, much to his delight, to get a yummy treat.

Dylan's Dog Squad

DEAR DYLAN'S DOG SQUAD

Dear Dylan's Dog Squad,

You talked to my class. Shelby is my dog. She is six and can't hear. Does she know I love her?

Allison
Winston Elementary School

Dear Allison,

We remember you! Thank you for writing.

Humans have five senses. They are taste, touch, smell, sight, and hearing Dogs have the same senses but they are a little different. Even though Shelby doesn't hear, she still has four other senses. Did you know a dog's sense of smell is its strongest sense? Experts guess it is 100,000 times stronger than a human's sense of smell.

Something tells me Shelby already knows you love her. To remind her, you can do these things.

Cuddle her.

Make eye contact when you want to get her attention.

Pet her. Dogs love to have their muzzles, ears and backs rubbed.

Play with her.

You and Shelby are lucky to have each other!

Dylan's Dog Squad

Dear Dylan's Dog Squad,

When I was growing up our family dog was a beautiful collie named Bella. We took good care of her, made sure she had a balanced diet, exercise, and got regular checkups from the vet. Then, one day, Bella was deaf. We were heartbroken and didn't understand what we'd missed or did wrong. Our vet explained Bella's deafness was caused by a congenital defect. There was nothing we could have done to prevent it. When Bella passed away, I swore no more dogs.

Then Max, a scrappy terrier mix—all skin and bones, showed up on my doorstep one day and refused to leave. I should find him a good home. I don't want to go through with Max what I went through with Bella. So now what?

Sincerely,
Peter

Dear Peter,

Surprise! Max has found a good home, yours. Sometimes you pick a dog and sometimes the dog picks you. So, to borrow from you, now what?

Even when we know the cause of our pet's illness, we can still feel bad. But the more you know the better your chances will be to help your dog receive the care he needs. If you suspect your dog is suffering hearing loss, please consult your veterinarian immediately to determine the best course of treatment. Sooner is always better than later.

Sometimes hearing loss is temporary due to wax buildup or debris in the ear and can be treated. Other reasons are more serious, such as tumors, ear infections, an accident, drug toxicity, nerve damage, ruptured eardrum, low thyroid disease, head injury or age related. These are serious conditions and expert advice is needed to ensure your dog gets the best treatment possible.

Probably the most common cause of hearing loss in dogs is age. Age related deafness usually happens at twelve years and older. This is considered normal aging and is often called sensorineural (sen so ri neu ral) hearing loss. (Consult your veterinarian for the technical details.) While this is upsetting for many owners, it is not harmful or fatal to the dog. Most normal aging hearing loss occurs gradually, and it is thought the dog doesn't notice. Even then many dogs may still hear high pitch sounds, such as a whistle or a doorbell.

If the hearing loss occurs suddenly, dogs have been known to panic or to feel anxious. Be careful when your dog is sleeping. If it is necessary to awaken him, stroke his back until he gradually becomes aware of you.

There are many things you and Max can do now to prepare for age related deafness. Start by learning American Sign Language and hand commands for Sit, Stay/Release, Down, Come, and Quiet. (Refer to Chapter Seven.) These can keep Max safe and are helpful to know even if he has not suffered a hearing loss. Remember to learn fun commands, too, such as Yay! Dylan's Dog Squad's favorite is I love you. Everyone should know that one.

Crate training if done properly (more on this in Chapter Seven) is also helpful should Max lose his hearing later. Max will come to regard his crate as a haven of safety, kind of like his own doggie clubhouse. So much so that he will go there on his own, just because. If Max knows he is in a safe, familiar place he will feel more secure and less lonely. If you have to leave him alone, don't forget to include his favorite toy!

Dylan's Dog Squad

Dear Dylan's Dog Squad,

While my friend is on temporary assignment for six months, I'm pup sitting her Russian Wolfhound. Nadia is a good girl and is about three years old. She's not crate trained—I doubt if there is one big enough for her. She sleeps on my bed and that's okay. I think.

My bed is a California King so there is plenty of room to spread out. Nadia insists on sleeping as close to me as possible. She also hogs the pillow. Sometimes I wake up and find myself barely on the bed. If I get up in the middle of the night she takes my spot. Is this Nadia's way of saying she doesn't she like me?

Carlos

Dear Carlos,

Nadia feels safe next to you. Dogs are naturally pack animals and her need to sleep next to you is a holdover from the wild. The pack gave them protection from predators and gave them emotional support from other members of the group. In this instance, you are the pack.

As for stealing your spot and your pillow, that's Nadia's way of saying she adores you. Being in your comfy spot is the next best thing to having you there.

Dylan's Dog Squad

DEAR DYLAN'S DOG SQUAD,

I met my dog Rocket when I rescued him from running alongside an interstate highway. He's thirty-five pounds, has a face only a mother could love, ears that don't match, striped and spotted fur, shorter legs in front and a tail like a metronome. People often study Rocket for a minute before giving up and asking what kind of dog he is. I used to answer, "Fast." There wasn't a hill too high to climb or a stream to wide to cross until he developed bone cancer in his right hind leg. The amputation was successful, and Rocket has adapted. Mostly.

Rocket can walk but he tires easily. I take him with me on car rides and every day we go to the park. He's happy to be there but when he sees other dogs run by, I can't help but feel sad for him. I wish I could do more.

Anastacia

DEAR ANASTACIA,

Good mommy!

Consider a dog stroller. There are a number of styles. Some have canopies which are useful on sunny or rainy days. Many have screens all around to keep Rocket in if he gets too excited or just needs a little me time to snooze. Look for ones that have places for bottled water, dog treats, supplies and toys. We suggest taking Rocket with you to try one out. It needs to be large enough for him to lie down and stretch out his left hind leg. You will want a comfy firm cushion to line the bottom of the stroller too. To keep the cushion clean and to keep Rocket from getting too hot put a towel on the cushion or put the cushion in a pillowcase. With a stroller you can enjoy long walks together or even jogging. Many businesses are agreeable to customers visiting with their pets if they are contained.

If you like to bicycle, consider getting a dog bike trailer for

Rocket. They are safe and screened in, so Rocket won't miss a thing. Remember to add a comfy firm cushion for your fellow traveler and his favorite toy.

These things can create a whole new world for you and Rocket. You are doing a great job and Rocket knows it.

Dylan's Dog Squad

DEAR DYLAN'S DOG SQUAD,

When I adopted Rufus from the shelter, he was three years old and deaf. The shelter didn't know what caused his hearing loss. Rufus has big floppy ears, and my vet thinks he might have had ear infections that went untreated. Rufus goes with me everywhere and is happy about everything in life. Even though he can't hear he always watches my mouth move when I'm talking and seems to regard what I'm saying. My friends think I'm crazy to keep talking to him.

Michael

DEAR MICHAEL,

Let them! It seems to us that you two have a special bond. (We think your friends are jealous.)

When you are talking to Rufus, you're paying attention to *him*. Even though Rufus can't hear you speak, he is paying attention to *you*. That's wonderful. This shows he trusts you and relies on you.

Dylan's Dog Squad

DEAR DYLAN'S DOG SQUAD,

One day when we were walking Lucy, our four-year-old Corgi, at the park, a boy went by on a skateboard. Lucy loves kids but to our surprise she snapped at him. About a week later we dropped a book next to Lucy when she was lying on the floor. She growled.

We took Lucy to our vet and our vet referred us to a specialist. We learned Lucy has about forty percent vision and it's like Lucy is seeing the world through a dirty window. The specialist prescribed drops and a follow up schedule but told us Lucy will eventually go blind.

Lucy must be so scared. What can we do to help?

Sincerely,
Max and Ramona

DEAR MAX AND RAMONA,

Sadly, many dogs lose their vision over time. When this happens, it is not unusual for a dog to feel isolated or anxious. Start training Lucy to be near you. Keep a lightweight, short leash on her at all times. When you move about the house, etc. take Lucy with you. She will like knowing you are near. Also, dogs like a purpose. Lucy will feel like she has a job to do.

Is Lucy crate trained? If not, see Chapter Seven. If you must leave Lucy alone, being in a crate with her favorite toys will help keep her calm and feeling safe. Some dogs like the TV on or music on when their owners are gone. When she is alone or evening comes, make sure bright lights are on. Even though Lucy sees very little, this will help a bit.

Include Lucy in daily life as much as you can. Dogs (like humans) have five senses: taste, touch, smell, sight, and hearing. Smell is the keenest. Do you like to barbecue? I'm sure Lucy would like to join you when you do. Take short car trips around town, leaving the window down—*no more than three inches,* so she can capture the smells along the way. She will start to associate certain smells with locations. Make sure Lucy is wearing a crash tested harness and is secure in a car seat. If you are in a public place, such as the car wash or the park, be quick to warn people that Lucy is blind and not to approach. You don't want to take the chance that she will startle and snap. Invest in a dog stroller. Dogs love a good ride. Many businesses are accepting of dogs if they are suitably confined. A stroller will keep Lucy safe, and she will be included in your daily activities.

Lastly, make sure Lucy has your contact information on her collar and she is microchipped. If she should get lost, these things will be helpful to ensure her return.

You and Lucy can do this.

Dylan's Dog Squad

Dear Dylan's Dog Squad,

I'm a responsible guy so I went to a local shelter and picked out a dog. Sigmund is some sort of dog.

Anyway, I knew there would be fees involved but I was shocked to see a fee was included for neutering. I explained I wouldn't breed Sigmund so why should he have to undergo a useless surgery?

How can I get out of paying the fee?

*Signed,
Gilbert*

Dear Gilbert,

No owner wants his pet to undergo a surgery. However, the American Society for the Prevention of Cruelty to Animals (ASPCA), estimates 920,000 shelter animals are euthanized each year.

As a responsible guy, stop for a moment and think. You are getting Sigmund from a shelter. That means Sigmund was abandoned or relinquished. With so many dogs in shelters, not all can get adopted. For the ones who can't get adopted their fate is worse than a simple surgery.

Do the right thing.

Dylan's Dog Squad

Dear Dylan's Dog Squad,

Our son found a Golden Labrador by a dumpster during a rainstorm and brought her home. She was half-starved and badly beaten. We named her Hope.

The vet guessed Hope was about five months old. Hope has now been with us for six months and has thrived. You would never know she had a sad beginning except for her reaction to water in general. We live on Lake Washington, and she refuses to go anywhere near the lake. (We are okay with that.) She also dodges puddles on the sidewalk and won't even step on the grass if it is a little bit wet.

Rainy weather is coming soon and that means thunder and lightning too. Because of Hope's history we're concerned she may not want to go outside—even to go potty. Our vet suggested giving her a mild sedative to keep her calm during a storm. What else can we do to help her?

Thank you,
Lou and Rhonda

Dear Lou and Rhonda,

We suggest getting an easy up tent or pop-up tent for your backyard. (The kind you see vendors use at fairs or people use to keep guests cool during the summer.) The tents come in a variety of sizes and colors and take less than five minutes to put up. Put it in Hope's designated potty area to introduce it to her now. She will get used to seeing it and won't be frightened by something new during a storm.

An indoor treadmill is a good idea too and the treadmill can be used year-round. The idea is for Hope to get enough exercise so she will feel relaxed and calm before a storm. Set the treadmill for a natural walking pace, this is not the Boston Marathon. Get on the treadmill and place Hope on the walking portion, between your legs. Until she gets used to the treadmill limit your walks to five or ten minutes. Never leave her unattended on the treadmill. Don't be surprised if she still wants to hop on in good weather. Dogs love treadmills and will actually become addicted to them, hopping on all by themselves.

Prior to a storm take Hope out for a long walk or for a fast game of fetch. You want to wear her out so she will feel relaxed and calm. Plan to stay inside during the storm and occupied by a relaxing indoor activity, such as watching a movie. Make it a festive occasion complete with every dog's favorite snack, popcorn! Just remember to make it plain or air-popped popcorn and only give it to Hope in moderation. During the storm keep her calm by slipping two fingers under her collar and keeping her close. Praise her frequently. When it is time for bed soothing music on low is helpful, too.

Let us know how you do!

Dylan's Dog Squad

Dear Dylan's Dog Squad,

Samantha is part Greyhound. She had hip surgery three days ago and is now wearing the plastic "cone of shame" until her incision heals. I understand this is necessary to keep her from licking the area, but Samantha is having way too much fun with this. She has taken to charging past us and has managed to scrape skin off every leg of every member of the family—at least once. When she is sitting next to us, she will suddenly swing her head around and clobber us with the cone. She always gives us an innocent face, but she doesn't look that sorry about it. We think it's her way of getting even.

Help,
Regina

Dear Regina,

Sounds like payback to us too. During the day when you can watch her, you might try letting Samantha wear a child's pair of shorts. The shorts will need to be snug enough to cover the incision so she can't get to it but loose enough not to cut off circulation. You may have to adjust the length so she doesn't trip when she runs or walks. Of course, take it off when she needs to go potty.

Also ask your vet about the *soft* cone of shame. If your vet agrees, the soft cone can be purchased from a local pet store. The soft cone isn't as hot as the typical plastic cone, it can be washed and your body parts will remain unscathed. Dogs are pretty clever about getting to areas they shouldn't, so Samantha should definitely wear the plastic cone at night until your vet says otherwise.

Dylan's Dog Squad

DEAR DYLAN'S DOG SQUAD

Dear Dylan's Dog Squad,

Ever since my twin seven-year-old daughters could talk they have been pestering me for a dog. I like dogs but I thought the girls were too young. I managed to hold them off until a friend showed up on our doorstep at the beginning of summer with Miss Dixie, an apricot Poodle. In front of my daughters my friend explained that her grandmother had to go into a nursing home and couldn't take Miss Dixie with her. Great. Miss Dixie moved in.

She's wonderful. The girls are delighted. They had tea parties and Miss Dixie was the honored guest. They had fashion shows and Miss Dixie was the star and wore a tiny tiara. Neighborhood kids came over to play and Miss Dixie joined in. It's as if Miss Dixie has always been in our family.

School started last week. I drove the girls to school and Miss Dixie came along for the ride. When the girls got out Miss Dixie looked out the window, pawed the window frantically, and started to whine. And kept whining all the way home. At home she refused to eat or play with her toys. She just stayed curled up in her basket. When I picked up the girls from school Miss Dixie launched into a doggie rhumba as if they'd been parted for a week. The same thing happened the next day and the next. Only now, Miss Dixie seems sadder while the girls are in school, as if that's possible.

I talked to our vet, and he explained that Miss Dixie is going through separation anxiety and suggested medication. This seems a little extreme. Can I try something else first?

Bette

Dear Bette,

By now Miss Dixie knows the daily routine and she knows she's not part of it. All dogs need a job, a purpose. For an entire summer (which is a very long time to a dog), Miss Dixie has been the center of your girls' world and she theirs.

The next time you take your girls to school do not go home right away. Take Miss Dixie to the park or take her to run errands with you. Try enrolling her in a basic training course so that she can interact with other dogs. Or try an Agility Training course, something that will stimulate her and wear her out. Contact your local pet store and see if they offer a Therapy Dog Training Program. Miss Dixie sounds like a happy dog with a lot to give. She might enjoy sharing her love with others while her favorite girls are at school. If Miss Dixie's routine is varied, she won't be able to anticipate the hours of being alone at home.

If none of this works, it is time to see your vet again.

Dylan's Dog Squad

NINE

FOREVER IN OUR HEARTS

Dear Friends,

Words fail when it comes to offering comfort to one who has lost their dog. It doesn't matter if the dog was sick or injured, old or in poor health.

Be the good friend that you are and listen with an open heart. Advice isn't necessary, wanted or needed. Your friendship is more than enough.

Dylan's Dog Squad

DEAR DYLAN'S DOG SQUAD,

Everyone says their dog is the best and it's true. I know because my dog Rambo was the best.

Because of my job I have to fly to the East coast twice a month. Rambo could never go with me, but I always made sure he was taken care of by someone he knew and loved. Just before my last trip I could tell he was slowing down. Our vet said it was old age. Rambo was thirteen and that's a lot for a black Labrador. Still, he enjoyed his walks, ate like a champ and played a mean tug of war.

When I returned from my trip three days later, Rambo couldn't get out of his bed. I was told he hadn't eaten all day and wouldn't drink water. I immediately took Rambo to the vet, and he passed away on the examining table. I went to pieces. I couldn't believe my best friend was gone. Even now I think I see him or hear him. If I had known those were his last days, I wouldn't have gone on the trip. I feel so guilty.

Merrick

DEAR MERRICK,

Dogs love a job, and they love to please their humans. For thirteen years you were Rambo's job. Part of his job was to wait for you to come home. When you did, he knew he could leave you. True friends are never forgotten, and you will never forget him.

Dylan's Dog Squad

DEAR DYLAN'S DOG SQUAD,

We think our mother loves her dog Tommy more than she loves us kids. We'd be hurt by that, but Tommy is a really, really great dog. Our dad passed away two years ago and now that we're out of the house, we're glad she has Tommy to fuss over. He keeps Mom busy and because of him she gets exercise.

The thing is, Tommy is about seventeen. Mom always jokes that they are both getting on. Tommy can't live forever, and we're concerned what will happen to Mom when that awful day comes. Can you give us some advice to ease her pain?

Sincerely,
Toby, Maria, and Gina

DEAR TOBY, MARIA AND GINA,

If only it were that simple.

While you can't prepare for the sadness that will surely follow Tommy's passing, perhaps you can prepare some keepsakes for your Mom now. Since Tommy is such a wonderful little guy, we're betting he's had his photo taken many times over the years. Talk to your siblings and see who has photos of Tommy. Have someone take charge of organizing them into a photo album. The next time you are all together pose for a family photo. Be sure Tommy is sitting front and center!

Find your mom's favorite photo of Tommy and put it on a T-shirt; tote bag; coffee mug; garden flag; throw blanket; custom jewelry, such as a necklace, earrings and bracelet; windchime or memorial garden stone. An engraved key chain or 3D crystal tributes are nice too. Search the aisles of your local craft stores for other ideas such as a DIY pet pawprint Christmas ornament kit.

When the time comes your best gift will be your love.

Dylan's Dog Squad

Dear Dylan's Dog Squad,

I live in a canyon and that means I'm surrounded by nature. Something is always growing and something is always blowing in the air. During allergy season Humphry would get the sniffles and occasionally took allergy medication.

One day he was sneezing more than usual. The earliest appointment we could get was that evening. Humphry ate his dinner, played with his toys and even had two tablespoons of vanilla ice cream. On the way to the clinic Humphry snoozed in his car seat and snored. I thought of canceling the appointment but decided to keep it.

Because it was during Covid I had to remain in the car while Humphry was examined. About an hour later the vet called, told me Humphry had a massive tumor on his spleen, and it was inoperable. He had maybe a few hours.

I was so stunned I asked if she had the right dog. I had been only expecting a change in Humphry's medication. Then I demanded to go in and see him.

When the technician brought Humphry to me his body felt like it was on fire. He was in extreme distress and was panting. The vet gently asked me about euthanasia. I felt like my heart had been ripped out but when Humphry looked up at me, I saw the answer. I couldn't make him better but I could make it so he didn't hurt. Humphry gave me one last look, heaved a sigh and passed away in my arms.

I know I should feel lucky to have had Humphry for sixteen years, but it just wasn't long enough.

Tess

DEAR DYLAN'S DOG SQUAD

Dear Tess,

It's never long enough.

Just know that although you didn't have Humphry all your life, he did have you for all of his.

Dylan's Dog Squad

ABOUT DYLAN EASTER TROY

Dylan was born on Easter in Daejeon, South Korea. His owner bought him from Walmart. At that time, I suggested basic dog training, but his owner didn't think training was important. Dylan immediately destroyed his owner's apartment by chewing his way through electrical coverings, baseboards, and furniture. When Dylan ate the interior of his owner's BMW, his owner decided having a dog was too much work and didn't want him anymore.

I said I would take him.

Dylan spent twenty-seven hours in a plane's cargo hold to get to California. When I picked him up at Korean Air Cargo, Los Angeles International Airport, he was eighteen months old, didn't know his own name, and was not housebroken. We immediately started training and Dylan thrived. He loved agility training and competing with other dogs. His first big step came when he became certified as a Therapy Dog. Dylan enjoyed that job but when he became American Kennel Club Canine Good Citizen certified, he went into service dog training and became a Hospice Service Dog for people actively dying.

Additionally, Dylan's accomplishments include:

- Bilingual understanding: English and Korean
- Five hundred word and phrase vocabulary
- Basic American Sign Language and hand commands
- Ability to contact 9-1-1 with a special device
- Count to ten
- Television appearances
- Recognized in a feature article in *The Orange County Register* for his accomplishments
- Recognized by Baskin-Robbins for his accomplishments and his love of their vanilla ice cream
- Mascot for Cypress College in Cypress, California

Dylan is proof that there are no bad dogs. In fact, he's the smartest, best dog I've ever had or trained. Dogs need love, guidance, companionship, and a sense of purpose. At the end of Dylan's workday, he received a bit of Baskin-Robbins vanilla ice cream.

He deserved it.

ACKNOWLEDGMENTS

A very special thanks to Teri Vitters, dear friend and gifted fellow writer. One day we met for lunch at Cedar Creek, our favorite restaurant. We used the first ten minutes to catch up on the latest (we see each other all the time) and then immediately launched into what we were writing. Teri was finishing her young adult novel *Pigeons on the Roof* and would soon begin querying agents. I told her I had begun *Dylan's Millions*, the sixth book in the Dylan's Dog Squad series but I had an idea for a nonfiction book called *Dear Dylan's Dog Squad*. Since I'd never written nonfiction before I was a little concerned. What should it look like? What topics should I address? Teri, being a devoted mom to two Yorkies and one Shih Tzu Maltese, immediately jumped in with enthusiasm and great advice. Thanks to Teri, when we parted I had a clear vision of what to do. Two months later, *Dear Dylan's Dog Squad* became a reality.

It's a fact: Dog people are generous and supportive. When I was researching topics for *Dear Dylan's Dog Squad*, I sought advice and wisdom from national and local organizations such as the ASPCA (American Society for the Prevention of Cruelty to Animals), Humane Society, Sunny Saints Southern California St. Bernard Rescue, German Shepherd Rescue of Orange County, and Mutts in Need. In each instance I was greeted as if they were just waiting to hear from me. I can't thank them enough for the work they do, the help, assistance, and education they provide, as well as their tireless efforts to provide forever homes to all the animals they serve.

A very special thank you to Jynafer Yanez, creative consultant and modern-day Wonder Woman. You work tirelessly to champion my dreams. Thank you for changing my life.

Many thanks to Jonathan and Jynafer Yanez, Archimedes Books Imprint, for providing publication, distribution, and social media assistance. You are truly amazing, and I am grateful for you every day.

Many thanks to my best friend Robyn Matias for her constant support and never telling me once that I should stick to my day job.

Many thanks to Deborah Halverson and her invaluable editing comments. You are always there when I need you. *Dear Dylan's Dog Squad* is the eighth book we have worked on together. When you return my manuscript with suggested revisions, I always feel that it is like opening the best gift under the Christmas tree.

I couldn't have done any of this without you.

ABOUT THE AUTHOR
KATHLEEN TROY, JD; PHD

Kathleen Troy is a published author, children's book publisher, movie producer, writing and law professor at Cypress College, and former Director of Education and Development for the Archdiocese of Los Angeles. Kathleen is an active member of Sisters in Crime and Society of Children's Book Writers and Illustrators and has won several awards for middle grade and young adult books. Dog training is Kathleen's passion, and she has achieved recognition, most notably for training service dogs for hospice work.

Kathleen welcomes hearing from you. Please get in touch with her at www.kathleentroy.com.

STAY INFORMED

I'd love to stay in touch! You can email me at kathleen@kathleentroy.com

For updates about new releases, as well as exclusive promotions, visit my website and sign up for the VIP mailing list. Head there now to receive a free story

www.kathleentroy.com

Enjoying the series? Help others discover *Dear Dylan's Dog Squad* by sharing with a friend.

www.ingramcontent.com/pod-product-compliance
Lightning Source LLC
Chambersburg PA
CBHW020248010526
44107CB00002B/154